Diary of a Dismissed Delegate:

Public Good at the Mercy of Bureaucracy and Sycophancy in Cameroon

Mwalimu George Ngwane

Langaa Research & Publishing CIG
Mankon, Bamenda

Publisher:
Langaa RPCIG
Langaa Research & Publishing Common Initiative Group
P.O. Box 902 Mankon
Bamenda
North West Region
Cameroon
Langaagrp@gmail.com
www.langaa-rpcig.net

Distributed in and outside N. America by African Books Collective
orders@africanbookscollective.com
www.africanbookscollective.com

ISBN:9956-763-08-X

Praise for this Book

"*Diary of a Dismissed Delegate*" is an epitome of a 'system'; I dare not call it, the government that exists in Cameroon. The diary succinctly unveils the inner workings of a system that thrives on political patronage wherein clientelism supersedes merit, and where the quest, conquest and consolidation of political power by all means relegate hard work, steadfastness and truth to the background. There are many Cameroonian civil servants who have silently suffered, and who continue to endure what befell Mwalimu George Ngwane. "Diary of a Dismissed Delegate" is an unbiased narrative based on well documented evidence. In the book one can see how patriotism, love for motherland and development embodied by the writer have been sacrificed by those who are politically selfish and have no fear for the judge of the supreme court of conscience. At the end of a piece that kept me spellbound in a straight read, I came away with the impression that the Mwalimu is considering putting an end to his writing simply because his 'writing mates' have stopped writing or have moved on to other activities. I just hope I got this wrong! When a writer stops writing, he stops living! Long live the Mwalimu's pen! I am looking forward to another incisive piece from Mwalimu George Ngwane sooner than later.

Tehwui Lambiv
Senior Journalist
Cameroon Radio and Television and
Lecturer, Advanced School of Mass Communication
University of Yaounde II

This is an interestingly revealing and a candid reflection of the plight of intellectual honesty versus blackmail and injustices. It is a vivid picture of a true servant of the people against sellers of political illusion. In his characteristic style, George Ngwane paints mind-searching narratives where patriotism and pretence are at daggers drawn; and where inspiration and greedy ambitions clash. This beautifully crafted book will surely expand your space of freedom of expression and render you a servant of the people in a society where many and sundry prefer silence for position, even at the rape of their trappings. It is a document for every good coach and mentor of exemplary patriotism. Why not title it a *Diary of a God-appointed crusader against injustices and corruption?* At the end of it all, principles will always prevail over shallow political blackmail and intrigues.

Professor Willibroad Dze-Ngwa
Historian and Political Scientist
University of Yaoundé I

In this *Diary of a Dismissed Delegate,* Mwalimu George Ngwane, recollects his short foray into the corridors of the Cameroonian *system* marked by its bureaucracy, sycophancy and the not less enticing comfort zone of the civil service elite. No one who reads this compelling narrative and who knows the Mwalimu would be surprised that it took so short for the contradictions of the system with his innermost principles and passion as a writer crusader for justice and the Anglophone cause could hardly have lasted longer. One is even amazed that neither the then Cultural Adviser at the South West Governor's office nor the others who tried to lure him to the other side knew better. His many essays and books on the political impasse in Cameroon and the marginalisation of the Anglophone were already there to attest to his integrity and dogged determination. That he accepted to serve as a Delegate of Culture may seem to be a departure from his true self but when one looks at the agenda he set for himself, one sees a passionate professional who would have revolutionised the promotion of culture not only in the South West but across all of Cameroon. In his hands culture would have become a veritable economic good from which artists, writers, musicians, curators, performers and actors would be earning income enough to take many families above the poverty line. It would also have been the tool through which the pan Africanism which Mwalimu champions through his NGO *AFRICAphonie* would have taken root at the grassroots and had visibility that comes through the very expression of our Africanness through untainted art. But what ultimately strikes one in this Diary is Ngwane's sincerity with his convictions. When he says that if another appointment came calling he would not say no, he is being honest about his right, like any other civil servant who deserves it, to be promoted and allowed to contribute, but it is also certain that he would remain true to himself as a crusader for genuine African democracy, equity for the Anglophone in Cameroon and the promotion of culture that takes Cameroon beyond 2020 through 2035 to veritable and enduring development with a space for all to live in prosperity and harmony. The Mwalimu we know will never be gagged by intimidation or the comfort zone of political appointment!

Vincent Anu
Coordinator Nkong Hill Top Association for Development (NADEV), Cameroon.

Foreword

When I received a tersely worded email from Mwalimu George Ngwane requesting me to write a foreword for this book *Diary of a Dismissed Delegate*, I was a little befuddled, wondering what could be so important in a diary kept by a civil servant who had a duty post that he held for only three months.

I opined that, in developed or better still in civilized societies, the public service is not a particularly lucrative, let alone an exciting sector. What with varying tales of manipulations, backstabbing, and cronyism that besmear the sector! So what was Ngwane up to? Chronicle his frustrations and whip up sentiments in his favour for a lost appointment? Was he going to cry over spilt milk in the hope of regaining hierarchical trust without compromising his stand on issues of public discourse?

Knowing Ngwane as a consummate and purposive writer and one who has a passionate and tenacious commitment to his convictions, I was convinced it will not be a sloppy and boring account of his disillusionment at the Ministry of Culture. So my perplexity soon gave way to curiosity. And as I later found out, the book which is introduced as Ngwane's reminiscences of his short- lived rise from a college teacher to a Provincial (Regional) representative of the Ministry of Culture in the South West Region, does indeed, exemplify the desperate condition of the Cameroonian civil servant who is called upon to work more under "control, command and intimidation" than his conscience and creative ability.

Ngwane's beliefs and writings may be at variance with the established order of things as argues Charles Nkongho, who maintained that " there is one cardinal role of politics; that if you want to criticize the government or political party, then you should not be in that government. Mr Ngwane's ideas may be great and progressive but once he has been appointed to a political post; he cannot use that platform to bite the finger that feeds him"

True, but only if one places personal interest above the general good. And here the question of patriotism and service to one's nation which I consider central theme of the book is fervently evoked. Which is better for a patriotic citizen: to accept to serve within a system whose flaws one knows but is blackmailed from denouncing it, or to work within that system and making sure one speaks out against the ills, even at the cost of your job, proposing and propounding theories and measures aimed at reforming that system?

Ngwane responds by juxtaposing "patriotism with pretence, inspiration with ambition, power of the pen with passion for profession and creativity with career mobility". He thus positions himself above the typical self-serving hypocritical Cameroonian by choosing patriotism over pretence and a creative mind over career growth that bleeds his conscience. Samuel Goldwyn was certainly speaking to the Ngwanes when he said, "I don't want any yes men around me. Let every man tell me the truth even if it cost them their job." And John Milton, the English poet in *Areopagitica* confirms "give me the liberty to know, to utter, and to argue freely according to conscience, about all liberties."

In the same vein, Professor Tam David – West, former petroleum and steel Minister under former Nigerian President Shehu Shagari, admonishes every academic in government to be "analytical, unpretentious and give solutions to problems. He must not allow himself to be emasculated in government …."This book, like his other works, firmly puts Ngwane within this intellectual prism. It illustrates a consistency in his beliefs on issues and positions him among the very few Cameroonians who stand by what they say and speak out when it is necessary to do so. He thus remains a shining beacon in a community suffering from a siege mentality of silence by continuing to demonstrate his belief that the many problems facing this country can be solved through public discourse.

Another focus of the book which one can regard as secondary theme, is Ngwane's new found comfort zone of the private sector and particularly the civil society. Truly as they say, "nothing happens for nothing". Dismissing Ngwane as South West Delegate of Culture gave him room to nurture, mature and excel in his civil society activities – probably a more intimate and enduring contribution to humanity. His engagement with the civil society laid the groundwork for his crusading initiatives for positive peace, becoming Senior Chevening Peace Fellow, Rotary Peace Fellow and Commonwealth Professional Fellow - and enabling him further his studies in British and Thai universities – accolades that he might never have had if he remained as a hand clapper and political apologist that the public service enslaves most of its high standing personnel.

In addressing his commitment and convictions about the private sector and especially the civil society, Ngwane brings to the fore the extreme paranoia with which government or better still, the public sector views and treats the former. Through his many writings and now his increasing civil society activities, Ngwane has been led, one would say, by his inner convictions and outward realities to reach the ignorant, disciple his civil service saints of the system and as a result, galvanises and mobilises a new momentum that is already building a legacy that his heirs and the world would be proud of. As someone said "in the well-adjusted person the ego is the executive of the personality and is governed by the reality principle"

Therefore, it is appropriate in conclusion, to paraphrase that one-time American President Woodrow Wilson by saying that the likes of Ngwane are here in order to enable us live more amply, with greater vision, with a fairer spirit of hope and achievement. In this book, Ngwane displays vision, a fine spirit of hope and ultimate achievement. People like him in the words of this great American, "are here to enrich the world"

Ngwane, if we may reiterate is an accomplished writer; his style is simple and pedagogical, his narrative is engaging and his plot nicely sneaky. It is a must read for everyone interested in the struggle to impact positively on our public policies and services.

Chief Zachee Nzohngandembou
Publisher and Chief Executive Officer
Eden Media Group
Cameroon

I did not know that my activities as Senior Discipline Master and especially Coordinator of Cultural activities in Bilingual Grammar School Molyko, Buea had caught the attention of both school authorities and public opinion in the South West Region of Cameroon. It only became evident when in the year 2000, I bumped into Reverend Victor Ayuk, then Social and Cultural Adviser at the Governor's Office, South West Region in front of the newspaper kiosk at Independence Square in Buea and he asked me if I could fill the vacuum left by Mr. (Dr) Samuel Bokwe who had left the post of Provincial Delegate of Culture of the South West to become Member of Parliament for Meme Division. I knew appointments came through acquaintances because my consent was sought before being appointed Senior Discipline Master. But I was sceptical about a Provincial appointment knowing the other intrigues that go with it ranging from blackmail to political patronage. I was not a member of the ruling party and my critical stance on democratic development in Cameroon was well known to those who read newspapers, watched television or listened to the radio. I had already written three books that exposed the delicate bond between Anglophones and Francophones and I was one of the founders of the All Anglophone Conference of April 1993 where I served as Moderator and later Member of the All Anglophone Standing Committee. It was difficult to fathom that any government that is intolerant of dissenting views and voices would accommodate within her rang someone who had not displayed any iota of ruling party loyalty. But Reverend Ayuk was hell bent on getting me to understand that my values as a cultural practitioner at a time when South West needed a renaissance of artistic triumph far outweighed my realistic appraisals of my political pedigree and the government's legitimate canons of ruling party inclination. He requested and got my Curriculum Vitae (CV) three days later and I went about my normal duties in Bilingual Grammar School.

On 15 September 2002, I was appointed Vice Principal of the Anglophone section of the Government Bilingual High

School Kribi while Mr Ateba Davy Simon Jean Claude took up functions as interim Provincial Delegate of Culture for the South West. Thrown far away from the turf of provincial appointment meant others who had shown interest (and one of them was heading one of the Government Hotels in Limbe and had the overt support of the out gone Provincial Delegate) in the job as well as the presence of an interim meant there was a clear geographical but not necessarily physical advantage over my bid. And indeed there were physical forces that believed in my taking the job, one of whom was Mr Bernard Eko. I knew Mr Bernard Eko from a distance first as someone who was a radio broadcaster and then as a vocal elite of the development or lack of it of the South West Region. We met casually during South West Elite Association (SWELA) forums and engaged in meaningful conversations on Cameroon's democratic trajectory and the place of the South West in any new dispensation. Of course he was a keen fan of my intellectual contributions in every public domain. In mid-2003 while in Kribi I got a phone call from Mr. Bernard Eko who was then Private Secretary to the Prime Minister to the effect that their office had received my CV with a forwarding proposal from the office of the Governor of the South West for the post of a Provincial Delegate of Culture for the South West and wanted to know if I was interested in serving the people of the South West in this capacity. I gave my consent. I now knew matters had gone out of my control as the compelling forces of physical proximity were edging over the competing features of geographical space. Even though I was aware that things were heating up fast in my favour , even though I knew deep down that appointments in this country were not a do or die affair for me, although I was aware that appointments can be changed by a Secretary without the knowledge of his or her boss, although I had heard stories of appointment decisions being changed between the final signature and the radio announcement, I remained steadfast and optimistic and in July 2003 I started writing a draft of my personal manifesto and cultural vision for the South West as follows:

1) ZONES OF CREATIVITY in the South West

Zone	Focus	Strategy	Resources
Meme Division	Film	Involve state and non-state actors with social and traditional themes as local content	Municipal Councils headed by Kumba City Council
Fako Division (Buea)	Theatre/fashion designers	Involve non-state actors and University of Buea	Cultural entrepreneurs
Fako Division (Limbe)	Books	Involve book professionals	Corporations
Kupe Mwanenguba	Traditional dances	Traditional Authorities	Local councils
Lebialem	Painting/Sculpture/craft	Cultural Associations	Local chiefdoms
Ndian	Indigenous choral music	Cultural Associations	Corporations
Manyu	Music	Cultural practitioners	Local councils

2) Identify Cultural facilitators (Chiefs' Conference, Cultural Associations, Media, etc.)

3) Sensitise Chiefs on constructing Palace Museums, Art Galleries and Resource Centres

4) Identify areas for mural painting in halls and walls along the road

5) Promote Indigenous language teaching during third term holidays in various zones

6) Encourage inter-provincial cultural cooperation

7) Establish a three- year Provincial cultural policy

8) Come out with a Medley of Rhythms of traditional music from the South West and an Anthology of the history on the origin of tribes of the South West

9) Establish Award on the most cultural-sensitive division annually making such a division the cultural capital of the Province annually

10) Use Mountain Cameroon Race of Hope and National Days to promote cultural activities

11) Observe all culture-related days (World Book Day, World Music day, World Museum Day etc.) and celebrate them in different divisions of the Province

12) Identify cultural sites and make them tourist-friendly

13) Request some of the underused Government houses especially in Buea to be transformed into Art Galleries, public libraries or museums

14) Institute awards for artists (posthumous and the living)

15) Encourage local councils to establish Community libraries

16) Request for the construction of a Provincial Cultural complex in the South West

17) Encourage hotel owners and offices to buy works of art from cultural professionals in the province and display in their premises.

My personal manifesto and this cultural vision were informed by my conviction that culture should never be seen as an appendage to political triumphalism but as a way of life. It was born out of the mission that if politics has been left in the hands of politicians; culture should be the property of the people. It was inspired by Paul Biya's assertion that "at the cultural level, we intend to create a synthetic cultural identity and acquire a new cultural personality that will either be eclectic or not" and what Professor Achille Mbembe observes as "the commodification of culture as spectacle and entertainment" because to me, culture is indeed another form of service delivery founded on the bedrock of creative economy.

Coincidentally it was also during this period that I started writing my first draft of the seminal and controversial political treatise titled "Cameroon's Democratic Process, Vision 2020" which was later published in The Post newspaper in a serialized manner and in the Senegal-based publication CODESRIA bulletin Numbers 3 and 4, 2004. As the treatise was quite long for newspaper publication I had plans to serialize it into Parts 1 to 5 in The Post newspaper.

Let me say here that even though I was expecting the appointment as Provincial Delegate, I had not stopped writing for local papers and international journals. And this did not go down very well with Mr Bernard Eko who at one time called me to order since in his opinion the writings could jeopardize my appointment. Unfortunately when patriotism and pretence appear before the court of conscience, when inspiration and ambition become strange bedfellows, when the power of the pen and the passion for profession are at logger heads and when creativity and career mobility are on a collision course, one of them inadvertently becomes a victim of choice and a choice of circumstances. Why, I asked myself had I been identified as a potential Culture Administrator if not for the streaks of cultural traits in my character? I was not a painter; neither was I a musician or a curator. I was a writer and to the best of my knowledge that was the only parameter I could be judged to qualify for the Culture Administrator. Why then did I have to give up the very cultural material I was made up of? I accepted the post of Delegate because I knew I had the ability and capacity to showcase the cultural industry and enhance the creative economy of the Province. I did not accept the post to stifle my innermost writing skills and disconnect myself with the public in debates of our democratic development. Being a Delegate was a career but being a writer in politic was a passion. Could they have run into conflict? Yes and No, but a writer is a cultural professional no matter his or her writing or political leanings. He is a key and relevant stakeholder in both the cultural and political arena of society.

On March 6, 2004, I left Kribi for Kumba to visit my two children (Hansel Masango and Alain Muabe) who were attending the Baptist High School. After the visit, I retired to my Elongo Gardens Hotel room to have a quiet rest as I was to leave for Kribi the following day. At about 8.13pm I got a phone call from Dr. Sammy Besong of the Ministry of External Relations Yaounde informing me of my appointment as Provincial Delegate of Culture for the South West as per the 8.00pm newscast. Then call after call of congratulations confirmed Dr Besong's announcement until I thought of switching my phone so I could find time to sleep. But I had not yet called my wife who was also an English language teacher in Kribi to double check. She had not followed the radio news because as she confessed later on she was more excited breastfeeding our three months old daughter Edibe born on 26th December 2003 and watching Television. My news to her was only made more real when our neighbours and colleagues started trooping to the house for the traditional congregation called "congratulation feast". I dare say this spontaneous traditional "appointment warming event" was more out of the bond and cordial relationship our family had established just close to two years with Ngoye and Dombe neighbourhood in Kribi. Worshipping in the Catholic Church where French language was the only vehicle of communication and being part of socio-economic meetings called "Njangi" were great outlets to unwind and commune with a community that was wrongly or otherwise labelled for her notoriety in alienating non-indigenes. As for our colleagues in Government Bilingual High School I had quickly and easily warmed my way to their hearts with an astute Anglophone academic tradition I had instituted in the Form Two Anglophone section of the school and the epicurean home parties my family used to organise with neighbours and friends being our most welcomed guests. As Vice Principal I had instituted a form of Staff socials within the Anglophone secondary section with revolving hosting thereby creating a professional and social network every month. From a tourist point of view Kribi is a gem with a beautiful beach, glamourous hotels and plenty of sea food. But from the perspective of a permanent resident, Kribi can be a little less hospitable with voracious mosquitoes invading even the confines of mosquito nets, high cost of living as expected of high tourist cities and inadequate family residences as most of the real estate is in the form of hotels. My wife and I sometimes wonder how our young children survived the only means of transport (motor bikes) to school and back with the daredevil Rambo-inspired Bamoum bike riders. We sometimes wonder what it could have been spending another two years in a place where our traditional Anglophone food was a rare delicacy. Even though Kribi is awash with fish, fish is very expensive as Yaounde and Douala wholesale buyers purchase fish in great quantities and in prohibitive prices to the detriment of local consumers. How did my household survive the endemic malaria bouts from mosquitoes that danced around electric fans? How did we survive the scorching night heat even in the heart of the protracted rainy season? How did our new born Blessing Edibe who has been a blessing to herself and the family sleep when the days were as hot as the night? So in our hearts of hearts my appointment as Provincial Delegate of Culture was more of a relief to leave Kribi and return to the South West where I had spent twenty-five years of my working career and to Buea where we had started building our family house. That this return to source was through a career promotion was of course a real icing on the civil service cake.

MINISTERE DE LA CULTURE

REPUBLIQUE DU CAMEROUN
Paix – Travail – Patrie

ARRETE N° 003 /MINCULT DU 05 MARS 2004
portant nomination de responsables au Ministère de la Culture

LE MINISTRE D'ETAT CHARGE DE LA CULTURE,

VU la Constitution ;
VU le décret n° 97/205 du 07 décembre 1997 portant organisation du Gouvernement, modifié et complété par le décret n° 98/067 du 28 avril 1998 ;
VU le décret n° 97/207 du 07 décembre 1997 portant formation du Gouvernement ;
VU le décret n° 98/003 du 08 janvier 1998 portant organisation du Ministère de la Culture ;
VU le décret n° 2002/217 du 24 août 2002 portant réaménagement du Gouvernement ;

ARRETE :

Article 1er.- Sont, à compter de la date de signature du présent arrêté, nommés aux postes ci-après dans les Services Extérieurs du Ministère de la Culture :

DELEGATION PROVINCIALE DE L'ADAMAOUA

Délégué Provincial : Monsieur **MBON MEKOMPONG Emérant**, Professeur des Collèges d'Enseignement Général, précédemment Délégué Provincial de la Culture pour le Sud, en remplacement de Monsieur IYA OUSMANOU, muté.

DELEGATION PROVINCIALE DU CENTRE

Délégué Provincial : Monsieur **TONYE Michel Archange**, Cadre Contractuel d'Administration, précédemment Délégué Provincial de la Culture par intérim pour le Sud-Ouest, en remplacement de Monsieur ESSAMA ESSAMA Fidelis, appelé à d'autres fonctions.

SERVICE DU PATRIMOINE CULTUREL

Chef de Service : Madame **NNOMO ELA Pulchérie**, Inspecteur des Affaires Sociales, précédemment en service au Ministère de la Culture, en remplacement de Madame BINDZI MEWOLI.

SERVICES DU PREMIER MINISTRE
VISA
000389 05 MAR 2004
PRIME MINISTER'S OFFICE

DELEGATION PROVINCIALE DE L'EST

Délégué Provincial : Monsieur **BEDENGUE Robert**, Professeur des Lycées d'Enseignement Général, précédemment Chef de la Cellule des Etudes et de la Coopération, en remplacement de Monsieur NYOBE Jean Jacob, muté.

DELEGATION PROVINCIALE DU LITTORAL

Délégué Provincial : Madame **MANGA Salomé**, Conseiller de Jeunesse et d'Animation, précédemment en service au Ministère de la Culture, en remplacement de Monsieur ONDOA MENVOUTA, appelé à d'autres fonctions.

DELEGATION PROVINCIALE DE L'OUEST

Délégué Provincial : Monsieur **ATEBA Simon Davy Jean Claude**, Conseiller Principal de Jeunesse et d'Animation, précédemment Délégué Provincial de la Culture pour le Sud-Ouest, en remplacement de Monsieur HANS CHOKENG, appelé à d'autres fonctions.

DELEGATION PROVINCIALE DU NORD-OUEST

Délégué Provincial : Monsieur **WANG JOHNSON SONE**, Inspecteur de la Documentation, précédemment Chef de Service Provincial du Patrimoine Culturel pour le Nord-Ouest, en remplacement de Monsieur AYUK ITA EREM, appelé à d'autres fonctions.

DELEGATION PROVINCIALE DU SUD

Délégué Provincial : Monsieur **NYOBE Jean Jacob**, Professeur des Lycées d'Enseignement Général, précédemment Délégué Provincial de la Culture pour l'Est, en remplacement de Monsieur MBON MEKOMPONG Emérant, muté.

DELEGATION PROVINCIALE DU SUD-OUEST

Délégué Provincial : Monsieur **NGWANE Georges ESAMBE**, Professeur des Lycées d'Enseignement Général, précédemment Censeur au Lycée de Kribi, en remplacement de Monsieur ATEBA Simon Davy Jean Claude, appelé à d'autres fonctions.

Article 2.- Les intéressés auront droit aux avantages de toute nature prévus par la réglementation en vigueur.

Article 3.- Le présent arrêté sera enregistré, publié suivant la procédure d'urgence, puis inséré au Journal Officiel en français et en anglais./-

SERVICES DU PREMIER MINISTRE
VISA
000389 05 MAR 2004
PRIME MINISTER'S OFFICE

YAOUNDE, le 5 MARS 2004

LE MINISTRE D'ETAT CHARGE DE LA CULTURE

Ferdinand Léopold OYONO

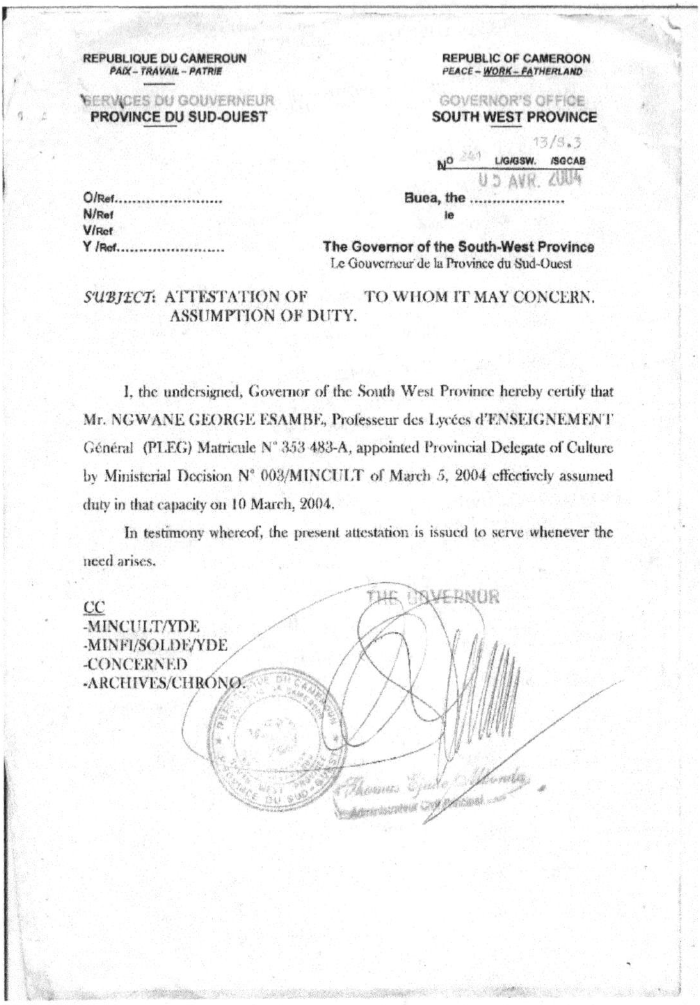

REPUBLIQUE DU CAMEROUN
PAIX – TRAVAIL – PATRIE

SERVICES DU GOUVERNEUR
PROVINCE DU SUD-OUEST

REPUBLIC OF CAMEROON
PEACE – WORK – FATHERLAND

GOVERNOR'S OFFICE
SOUTH WEST PROVINCE

13/S.3
N° 241 L/G/GSW. /SGCAB
05 AVR. 2004

O/Ref........................
N/Ref
V/Ref
Y /Ref........................

Buea, the ....
le

The Governor of the South-West Province
Le Gouverneur de la Province du Sud-Ouest

SUBJECT: ATTESTATION OF ASSUMPTION OF DUTY.

TO WHOM IT MAY CONCERN.

I, the undersigned, Governor of the South West Province hereby certify that Mr. NGWANE GEORGE ESAMBE, Professeur des Lycées d'ENSEIGNEMENT Général (PLEG) Matricule N° 353 483-A, appointed Provincial Delegate of Culture by Ministerial Decision N° 003/MINCULT of March 5, 2004 effectively assumed duty in that capacity on 10 March, 2004.

In testimony whereof, the present attestation is issued to serve whenever the need arises.

THE GOVERNOR

CC
-MINCULT/YDE
-MINFI/SOLDE/YDE
-CONCERNED
-ARCHIVES/CHRONO.

Thomas Ejude Mbonda
Administrateur Civil Principal

As it was the tradition I left Kribi for Buea on March 8th 2004 to receive the baton of a newly appointed Delegate. I assumed duty with all the low-key office fanfare on March 10th.

A few days after my commissioning as Delegate, Mola Loka Usman came to my office and told me he had been mandated by the late Paramount Chief S.M.L Endeley to inquire if I was a card-carrying militant of the Cameroon Peoples Democratic Movement (CPDM) the ruling party. I told him I was neither a member of the C.P.D.M nor the Opposition nor any political party for that matter. I did not bother to double check if Mola Loka Usman was indeed an envoy of the Late Paramount Chief even though I know he is very close to the Chief's Palace since he acts as the griot blowing his bugle in traditional and national occasions in Buea.

My first public duty and outing as Delegate was the burial of the South West musician, Sammy Mafany on March 16th. Sammy Mafany of the "ngoma-wetuli" fame died a few days before my appointment. I had known Sammy Mafany since when I was in the University of Yaounde in 1980. He was not only a personal friend who had been introduced to me by my late cousin Etub'Anyang, the famous Cameroonian country and folk musician but one who with late Francis Ndom and Etub'Anyang gelled as a new generation of Anglophone musicians holding their mettle and art in the rough and tumble music competition among Francophones in Yaounde. The trio represented the future of musicians west of the Mungo especially as both Sammy and Francis were members of the National Orchestra. It was therefore with pride that Anglophones would watch Francis do his "njang" dance from the North West, Sammy do his 'ngoma-wetuli" or shoulder dance from the South West and Etub'Anyang blend country and folk with Eurocentric inspiration against an exceptional patriotic and indigenous melody. I remember how I was called by Etub'Anyang to act as Impresario during one of the trio's performance in the French Cultural Centre Yaounde when the veritable Events maestro and radio journalist Muema Meombo was unavoidably absent. As impresario and friend I got to be close to Sammy and so his death was both a personal and official loss to me. Sammy was a likeable character, always with a summer smile on his face, a spring in his step and a mouth full of fertile conversations on music. How come that destiny could afford to play this trick on me as one charged with arranging his official burial from the Mungo bridge to Buea on that fateful March 16th? Luckily my work had been cut out for me by the ebullient Bernard Eko, the generous Mbella Moki who was the incumbent Mayor, my supportive office staff, my reliable Musicians of the South West and an empathetic leader of the Ministry of Culture delegation, Dr Raymond Asombang. After the burial I decided to spend a couple of days in Buea trying to acquaint myself with office chores and most especially tidying up the loose ends of my political treatise "Cameroon's Democratic process". I loved this treatise after reading it the way the late activist Steve Bantu Biko of South Africa loved his column "I write what I like" or what the late Zimbabwean writer Yvonne Vera once asserted during a writers' session she moderated in the hey days of the Zimbabwe International Book Fair in 1999. During that session I asked her what she thought about her writings which some people found offensive. She said "I write first for myself before my audience". Satisfied with the objectivity and thoroughness of the political treatise I went straight to the office of The Post newspaper and handed it to Pegue Manga who was then the Desk Editor of the paper. That was on the 10th of April 2004. Contrary to some public opinion that has accused the "Graffi" boys in The Post newspaper for "planting" the serialized article in the newspaper in order to expose me to administrative sanction barely two weeks after I had taken office as Delegate, let me make it crystal clear that I literally pressured the Desk Editor Pegue into publishing it. Pegue was my former literature High School student in Bilingual Grammar School Molyko with a deep knowledge of literary appraisal. After perusing the article he sensed that it could court trouble and tried to talk me out of publishing it at least for the sake of my job. My appraisal was different; my writings have always been pedagogic. In my judgment, my essays, most of which have animated debate and discourse in national newspapers, online blogs and international journals are lucid in their arguments, poignant in their ideological focus, rich in their non-fiction craftsmanship and urgent in their message delivery. Indeed one has to be in the head and mind of any artist or writer for that matter to understand the organic nexus between the artist's desire to expand his or her space of freedom of expression beyond the limitations imposed on us by our egosystem and the parochial judgments of our ecosystem. Society sometimes needs to understand how difficult it is for any committed cultural practitioner to escape from his or her vocation of communicating values however steeped they may be in restraint, respect and revolt. It is important for society to understand the dilemma of any artist who is a product of the dynamics of his or her society when faced with the challenge of striking a balance between message and mode, between confrontation and conformity and between defiance and dogma. It is true that the writer speaks on behalf of the speechless and amplifies the voice of the silent. We as writers often arrogate to ourselves the role of a compass directing the ship of state and society to the shores of sanity and holding high the flag post of freedom to the land of equal opportunities. Therefore since the writer does not impose his or her work on society, society should not impose their taste on the writer. In other words the debate should be about freedom of expression and freedom of consumption. The staff of The Post newspaper through its Executive Editor Francis Wache after reading Parts 1 and 2 of my article that appeared on April 19th and May 3rd 2004 requested that Parts 3, 4 and 5 be put on hold. I insisted to have them through with my knowledge that the full judgment, rationale and understanding of the treatise could best be appreciated only towards its finale the same way a reader or spectator of a Greek tragedy or Shakespearean drama appreciates the work of art only after reading or watching the five Acts. I was wrong; my Provincial hierarchy contented itself with reading only Parts 1, 2 and 3 not as students of political literature but as administrative henchmen. In fact a high profile Anglophone staff in the Governor's office went to the office of The Post newspaper pretending to be a voracious reader and requesting the copies of the newspaper which carried the articles. He then convinced the Governor to sanction me with a letter of Observation. As a writer in politics I wonder why the political elite underrate its structural violence on citizens and exaggerate the writer's intellectual violence on the regime. Anywhere I needed to rush back to Kribi to bring my family to Buea after all the office acquaintances. Getting the family settle down in Buea was quite easy. There was free lodging for the Delegate, the children enrolled in a beautiful Primary school which was a world apart from the crowded and the dilapidated classroom conditions in Kribi; the children were occasionally chauffeur-driven to school in the car of the Delegate-a far cry from the Bamoum motor bike riders' transport condition in Kribi. It was a break from a two year involuntary "national service" with all that it entailed to what could have been a protracted comfort zone where the perks of office were in consonance with personal inducement and financial sinecure. The government through this new appointment had like in every case of appointments of this category provided an enabling climate for career comfort and family security-the kind most Cameroonians would like to have and to hold for better or for worse till retirement do them part. And friends trooped my home and office with letters of congratulation.

George Ngwane appointed South West provincial delegate of culture

George Ngwane was last week appointed delegate of culture for the South West province. He replaces Samuel Bokwe Ngoe who is presently a member of parliament for Meme West.

George Ngwane

Before his appointment, Ngwane was vice principal of Government Bilingual High School, Kribi, a post he kept for a short time. He had also taught at Government High School, Mundemba and Bilingual Grammar school, Molyko, Buea – where he later became discipline master. Owing to the several years he has spent in the classroom as a teacher, Ngawne earned the title "Mwalimu" which means teacher in a Tanzanian language.

The new delegate is indeed a man of culture for he has written and published many books, one of which is read in a foreign university. He is equally the promoter of the Buea-based National Book Development council as well as a pan-Africanist movement known as Africaphonie. As a true pan-Africanist, he vowed many years ago never to dress in foreign attires as he used to do. Thus for many years running, he has been putting on only African wears.

Many people who know him and whom *The Herald* contacted, affirmed that the choice of George Ngwane as South West provincial delegate of culture was not a mistaken one.

Ndemba Emmanuel, taking care of prisoners' spiritual lives

After serving 15 years at the Kumba production prison, Ndemba Emmanuel is now determined to change the spiritual lives of inmates of the prison. Although while in the prison, he succeeded in changing the lives of 39 [illegible]tes bringing them closer to Christ, this time he says [illegible]'s to go into full-time evangelisation. He has in [illegible]

Jean Jacques Ndoudoumou

[illegible] intensified, to avoid poor selection and award. He told *Cameroon Tribune* on 9 March during a seminar to examine the situation of the award of contracts and actors involved that the law permits the prime minister to cancel any doubtful contracts.

It has been noticed that contracts are awarded to family members and friends who do not execute them after they had been paid. Ndoudoumou reassured that the situation had changed with the controls. He also said there had been cases where culprits of clandestine contracts have been sanctioned. "If you go to courts you see cases of people who have been sentenced for embezzlement or people who have won contracts clandestinely who have failed to execute them", he said. With this new lease in that sector it is believed that better public facilities in the country will soon be seen.

Eta-Besong Junior: Tipped as next *bâtonnier*

The allegations of rigging at the last Bar Council elections that eroded the credibility of the legal corps have led some reputable lawyers to begin reflecting on who should take the Cameroon Bar out of this mess. There is near consensus that only the leadership of a common law lawyer will help pick up the pieces. One of those who is being propped up as the next Bar Association president (*bâtonnier*) is Eta-Besong Junior, Buea-based lawyer known to be quite upright. Charles Taku, senior advocate at the War Crimes Tribunal in Arusha, Tanzania told *The Post* that Eta-Besong had the makings of good leadership that could take the Bar back [illegible]

Eta-Besong Junior

SM Mambanda to help the administrations of both schools renovate some dilapidated classrooms.

Palmy Nkele Mboe

The Kumba MP said the donation which was part of his parliamentary microprojects was geared towards raising the educational standards of young Cameroonians. He told the pupils and students to work hard because the future of Cameroonians was in their hands. He also told the teachers to perform their duty of moulding up the pupils and students to become better leaders tomorrow.

Receiving 75 sheets on behalf of his school, John Ebong, headmaster of GS Mambanda, hailed Nkele for the initiative, noting that it was the first time his school was receiving such a gift which came in timely.

For his part Peter Nganda, Principal of SAR-SM who received 150 roofing sheets described the donation as a dream come true. He pleaded for more of help in the construction of some classrooms in his institution.

Nkele's gesture, though small, has come in timely. With the rainy season at the corner, the roofing sheets will save the pupils and students the trouble of studying under leaking roofs.

Martin Abega, from BAT to GICAM

Martin Abega is the new secretary general of the Cameroon businessmen association -GICAM. He'll take over from Francis Sanzouango with effect from 1st April. Sanzouango will move to Geneva, Switzerland to take the post of coordinator for the Africa region at the international labour office.

Martin Abega

Before his new appointment, Abega was the communication director of British American Tobacco-BAT in Yaounde.

He has also been the general manager of *Trans Africaine* and editor in chief and publisher of *Africa Finance* magazine.

Now forty-four, Abega is a graduate of the [illegible]

C/O P.O Box 30234
Yaounde
Tel. : 231 31 87
17th March 2003

Mwalimu George Ngwane
Provincial Delegate for Culture
South West Province

Mwalimu,

LETTER OF CONGRATULATION

It was with a sense of immense joy and pride that we received news of your appointment as the Provincial Delegate of Culture for the South West Province.

AFRICAphonie since its inception has dwelled on the need for African Culture and Values to take their rightful place with regards to the quest for solutions to our identity, socio-economic and political problems amongst others. You in particular must be singled out for epitomising this resolve of ours by putting on an African outfit at all moments. In a Country where merit is not often given a chance; AFRICAphonie through my modest voice as one of the leading members considers your appointment as a very salutary move. The excitement that greeted your appointment from diverse quarters is an indication that you are indeed a square peg in a square hole. We are equally tempted to believe that the numerous activities carried out by our movement AFRICAphonie within the South West Province and at the National Level, must certainly have contributed in some way however remote to that recognition of merit in you.

The meaningful interactions that we have had over the years makes it convincing beyond reasonable doubts that you have what it takes to succeed in the execution of the arduous and challenging tasks of your new office. Hence before the dust settles, permit AFRICAphonie to add its humble voice to that of all your loved ones in saying congratulations !!!

We pray for your success and may the Almighty God be your guide.

Sincerely

MBAPNDAH AJONG

FORGET NOT

Be creative and norm-al

SUGGESTIONS BY POUBOM LAMY NEY

George,

What is a friend? One who minds and who reminds.... As you embark on your new job , here's my humble contribution:

1. Thank God.
2. Acknowledge to WHOM IT MAY CONCERN the confidence invested on you
3. master your job description
4. Master national requirements: policy, politics, official texts
5. Remember local exigencies and wishes: provincial, divisional... village
6. Note international and world contingencies
7. Conceive a plan of action : immediate – short – mid – long terms taking into consideration those of each and every department or service under you
8. contact colleagues (on retirement or not) with field experience
9. Empower collaborators
10. write out a succinct presentation of the provincial delegation

INNOVATE

1. Animate the Delegation by

   1.1 Keeping a TV set on a DVD running cassettes and CDs on Cameroon culture

   N.B Exploit the CRTV monthly competition, MMC in Yaounde, Roots by Alex Haley, THE TRIPLE HERITAGE.....

   1.2 Setting a show room for provincial culture productions

   1.3 Increasing Delegation space by building the Bakossi, Bakweri, Oroko.... Traditional houses

2. Beautify environment: flowers, south-west "country" houses, framing of posters of cultural events...., pictographism...

3. Each service presents in pamphlet form itself and all that is available for public consumption
4. Twinning of services : museum, archives
5. Boards for periodic cultural picture exhibitions (on theme???)
6. Seek partnership with:
   6.1. COUNCILS : Line of budget for culture, development of council libraries, council emblems and mottos, council museums……..
   6.2. VILLAGES : Village museums…. through concerned elites and associations
   6.3 Schools: clubs: dances………
   6.4 University : theatre arts, UNIFAC
   6.5 ASSOCIATION: SWELA, tribal groups
   6.6 MOUNTAIN RACE
7. Keep a catalogue of artists in your province:

- Painters	- Musicians
- Carvers	- Actors
- Writers	- Festivals
- Trade fairs	- Dances
- Meals	- Attires

8. Animate VIP (minister….) visits at Mungo Bridge and ceremonies
9. Mobile film showing in schools: documentaries, meaningful films…..
10. Give Meaning to the CCC (Cameroon Cultural Centre)
    - Snack
    - Library on Cameroon
    - Permanent film (documentaries) showing

BE PART OF

1. International, world, national, local days, weeks or Jubilees
   e.g - FENAC, FESTAC, UNIFAC
   - The slave Road project
   - The Africa child

2. Relationship with international organisation of interest:

It was under such a climate of office composure and serenity that I made this Flyer meant to showcase the Delegation of Culture and to be distributed to the end-users (the population).

KNOWING US, KNOWING YOU

We have published our Calendar of Activities that will spice and spur culture in the South West Province.

I) Open Day in Delegation of Culture with focus on the state and stakes of our Archives.
II) South West Cultural Awards with a view to compensating those that have been role models in the field of culture.
III) Seminars / Workshops on the film industry, book sector and musical research.
IV) Exchange Cultural Visits with other Provinces.
V) Erection of the Kuva Likenye monument.
VI) Cultural Fairs in all major towns.
VII) Launching of publications in the areas of books and music of budding talents.

And More! More! More!

We conceive and our partners concretise

We dream and you make culture's dream come true.

Contact
- Box 50, Buea S.W.P
- Tel: 332 22 17
- Location: Court Junction - Buea

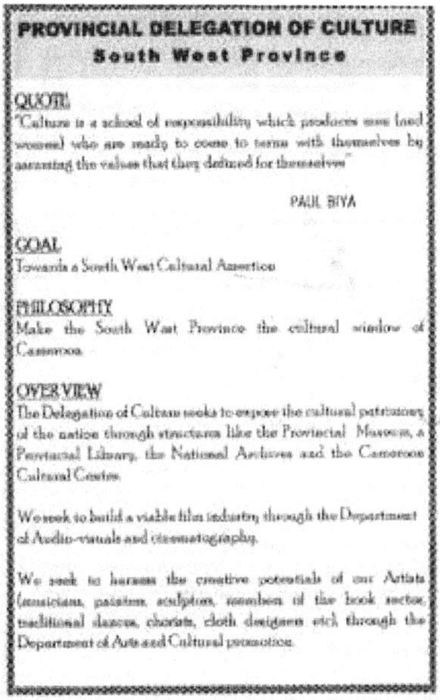

PROVINCIAL DELEGATION OF CULTURE
South West Province

QUOTE
"Culture is a school of responsibility which produces men (and women) who are ready to come to terms with themselves by accepting the values that they defined for themselves"

PAUL BIYA

GOAL
Towards a South West Cultural Affirmation

PHILOSOPHY
Make the South West Province the cultural window of Cameroon.

OVERVIEW
The Delegation of Culture seeks to expose the cultural patrimony of the nation through structures like the Provincial Museum, a Provincial Library, the National Archives and the Cameroon Cultural Centre.

We seek to build a viable film industry through the Department of Audio-visuals and cinematography.

We seek to harness the creative potentials of our Artists (musicians, painters, sculptors, members of the book sector, traditional dances, choirs, cloth designers etc) through the Department of Arts and Cultural promotion.

UNESCO, CICIBA..., COMMONWEALTH, FRANCOPHONE....

3. Competition on collections on cultural topics prior to events :

   e.g
   - Collection of provincial riddles
   - Collection of provincial proverbs
   - Collection of provincial folktales
   - Collection of provincial country people's names and meaning
   - Collection of provincial names of places + meanings
   - Collection of provincial legends and myths
   - ....

4. Advice to name places as a decent way to acknowledge and valorise local people : streets, school, libraries, junctions...
5. Proposals to build statues and portraits of historic figures
6. Concept of light publications on cultural landmarks in the province

   e.g
   - Epasa moto
   - The Mount Cameroon Race
   - Germans in S.W
   - Lake Barombi
   - Magic Stick
   - The Twin Lakes
   - Korup
   - The Left-Hand, or slaves in Mamfe
   - Know Akwaya
   - Customs (do and don't)
   - Country fashion
   - excision or female circumcision
   - ...

7. Conference
8. Collaboration with tourism
9. Animation of hotels: meaningful post cards, arts, exhibition and sales, dancing groups.....
10. Encouragement to cultural curators
    - Upholding national languages (see PMUC project)
    - Saving traditional sports and entertainments
    - Making and using traditional music instruments
    - Popularising traditional dressing styles

MAY YOUR DREAMS BE YOUR ONLY BOUNDARIES

With God on your side

POUBOM LAMY NEY
Cultural Curator
Chair: Comparative Africa Culture
And Primary Reading Care
B.P. 159
Tel: 332 25 89 / 985 43 14
Buea, Cameroon

A few weeks later I came out with the following Calendar of Activities for the Delegation of Culture.

Grassroots Grow

In the absence of Divisional Delegations, the Provincial body embarked, in the 80s, on a grassroots / people-oriented development strategy by creating a cultural Association in each division.

In Fako, there is the Fako Traditional Dance Association (FATRADANCA)

In Kupe Mwanenguba, there is the Kupe Mwanenguba Cultural Association (KUMUACULA),

In Lebialem, there is the Lebialem Cultural Association (LEBIACULA),

In Manyu, there is the Manyu Cultural Association (MANYUCULA),

In Meme, there is the Meme Traditional and Cultural Association (METRACULA),

In Ndian, there is the Ndian Cultural Association (NDIACULA)

Formerly, these Associations focussed mainly on traditional dances and choral groups, but a new policy designed by our Delegation since 2004 has widened the scope of the Associations to embrace all genres of Art hence the plan in 2005, to redynamise the leadership and change the appellation.

Grassroots Grow

Partnership Pays

The activities of these cultural Associations can succeed only through local sponsorship. Hence the need for Municipal councils, chiefs, MPs, business persons and commercial firms to lend financial assistance to these Associations. That's why we have launched a competition on "Cultural Division of the Year".

The Delegation of Culture has a triangular vision which is open to partnership ventures with all cultural operators.

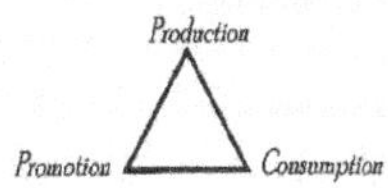

Our cultural projects are so attractive that any culturo-business partner would like to be part of our collective dream.

Who does not want "a hundred flowers to blossom so a hundred school of thoughts should contend".

Which business companies would want to stifle initiatives that enhance cultural development?

But beyond these aspects of promotion and production lies the very vexing question of consumption.

Why should the Delegation of Culture continue to showcase Artists whose products are rarely consumed by its people?

Why should our own media not place priority over our own indigenous culture?

We still believe in the adage "***Produce what you consume and Consume what you produce***".

Partnership Pays

PROVINCIAL DELEGATION OF CULTURE- S. W. P.BUEA

CALENDAR OF CULTURAL ACTIVITIES: 2004-2005

CODE	PROPOSED MONTH	NAME OF ACTIVITY	DETAILS	TOWN/DIVISION	OBSERVATION
A	April 23, 2004	World Book Day	Book Exhibition, children's book parade, panel discussion.	Buea Fako Division	Already done
B	May 13, 2004	World Museum Day	Painting, Sculpture, Arts exhibition visit of community museum.	Menji Lebialem	Already done
C	May 20, 2004	20th May festivities	Traditional dances, choral concert, painting, textile, book and craft exhibitions, discussions.	Buea Fako	Already done
D	May 26th, 2004	World Artist Day	Choral and Traditional Dance display; live Performance of 15 musicians.	Ekondo titi Ndian	Already Done
E	June 20, 2004	International Music Day	Traditional dances, choir, painting, live orchestra of 18 musicians	Tombel Kupe / Mwaneguba	
F	August 2004	Children's Book bazaar and games	Quiz, poetry, Reading and writing competition among children in primary schools	Buea Fako	

Code	Proposed month	Name of Activity	DETAILS	Town/Division	Observation
H	November 2004	Cultural Fair Panel discussion on the Buea Archives.	Display of Dance groups, choir and painters. Theatre Evening with Musinga group and Neighbours	Tiko Buea	
I	December 2004	Workshop on Media and Culture	Resource persons (Gwangwaa,Ngandembou, Kome Epule and Journalists (Participants)	Limbe Fako	
J	January, 2005	South West Cultural Awards (SWECA)	Awards to those who have contributed to the various areas of culture in the S.W. P. They act as role models to the young	Buea Fako	
K	February, 2005	Launching of Anthology on Folktales and legends of the South West	A call for especially unpublished writers to write on folktales, publishing after meeting with Editing committee	S. W	
L	February, 2005	Launching of a musical Album of medley of South West Music	A call for especially unproduced musicians to submit 2 songs each on purely tradimodern music of the South West People	S.W	
M	February 2005	Arts Fair	Exhibition and sales of Arts, Craft, Books,Textile, painting material on the eve of the **Mountain Race**	Buea Fako	

Code	Proposed month	Name of activity	Details	Town/Division	Observation
N	March 2005	Exchange cultural visit to West Province	Payment of transport and incentive to Bate Besong's theatre troupe to the university of Dschang (West Province)	Dschang West Province: Contact person; Delegate of West	
O	April 23 2005	World Book Day	Workshop with members of the Book sector in the S. W. P; meeting between Resource persons and participants	Mamfe Manyu	
P	May 13, 2005	World Museum Day	Painting, sculpture, dance and choral exhibition	Bangem Kupe/mwan	
Q	May 20, 2005	20th May celebrations Nakuve Memorial Documentary	Culture village, Nakuve memorial (paint bridge, erect monument and document with C.R.T.V.)	Buea Fako	
R	May 26, 2005	World Artist Day	Exchange cultural visit send painters/sculptors for Exhibition in Kribi with title " Painting on the Beach"	Kribi South Province Mayor of Kribi	
S	June 20, 2005	International Music Day	Exchange visit to Bamenda, send musicians to play in Bamenda	Bamenda N.W. Province Delegate of culture	
T	August 2005	Home Language Studies	Teaching during holidays of three S.W. languages to secondary students.	Buea Fako	

CODE	Proposed Month	Name of Activity	Details	Town/Division	Observation
U	October 2005	Cultural fair	Arts, craft, painting, Books exhibition and sale. Dance groups and choral festival	Limbe Fako	
V	November 2005	School Arts Competition	Cultural Competition among pupils /students in Schools in Mundemba	Mundemba Ndian Division	
W	December 2005	Publication of Anthology And Musical medley	Launching of musical Album and Anthology of Books in Buea	Buea Fako	

[signature] George NGWADE

CONTACT ADDRESS:

PROVINCIAL DELEGATE OF CULTURE
BUEA, BOX 55
SOUTH WEST PROVINCE
TEL: 332 22 17 / 766 84 79

I will let these newspaper clippings tell the story of my implementing the Calendar of Activities

World Museum Day celebrated in Lebialem

By Anu Michael

South West Delegate of Culture,Ngwane George, D.O. Fontem, Mayor and participants at the World Museum Day celebrations

More than 1000 people from all the nooks and crannies of Lebialem Division turned up at the Menji Municipal Stadium on May 13, 2004 to meet with the new Provincial Delegate of Culture for the South West Province, Mr. George Ngwane and to celebrate activities marking the World Museum Day.

The activities began at midday with the singing of the National Anthem in the *Nweh* language followed by a welcome speech by the Mayor of Menji Rural Council Mr. Nkemabin Mbiaoh Francis. The Lord Mayor thanked the Provincial Delegate for practicing the culture of proximity which enable the battery of culture persons in the division to commune physically with the Delegate and to enhance the trend of cultural awareness inherent in the Lebialem kith and kin.

Mayor Nkemabin told the gathering that it was not a mistake for the Provincial Delegate of Culture to have chosen his constituency as the site for celebration of the World Museum Day since the division not only produces rich art but has a history of conserving artifacts as old as 600 years in some of the palace museums. Testimony to this fact, the mayor continued, was the presence at the Menji stadium of more than 32 sculptors who had come to showcase their ingenuity and creativity.

Taking the rostrum after the mayor, was the president of Lebialem Cultural Association (LEBIACULA), Ndi Nwetbefua who not only appealed to all artists to register with the association and affiliate with the Delegate for culture but urged the Ministry of state for culture to build a community museum or Art Gallery in Menji.

In response to the welcome addresses, the Provincial Delegate for Culture, Mr. George Ngwane explained the objectives of his visit which were to compile a comprehensive list of Artists in Lebialem division, create a zone of creativity (sculpture) in the division, inform them of President Paul Biya's one billion grant meant to assist Artists and preside over the celebrations of the World Museum Day. Ngwane emphasized that culture was not just the preserve of the Ministry of State for Culture but a partnership venture with Municipal councils, Chiefdoms and the elite. Reason why the Delegate paid glowing tribute to Chief Fuatabong Acha Charles Taku, Ndi Nkemayang Paul and Ndi Nkem Atabong Augustine for responding to the letters of Appeal he had sent out to Lebialem elite before the World Musuem Day.

The speech making exercise was closed by the 2nd Assistant Senior Divisional Officer Mr. Derek Lokombe who then led the Provincial Delegate, Mayor the Divisional Officer and Provincial Delegate of communication to visit the Art and Craft exhibition mounted by more than 32 sculptors.

The World Museum Day and contact meeting of the Delegate of Culture in Lebialem ended with a mountainous journey to one of the best Museums in the Division- Fotabong-Anche Foundation Museum- Lewoh Palace

Tenants vs landlady in assault case

By Chipo Melo

A couple appeared before the Court of First Instance, Limbe for assaulting their landlady and her daughter in Bobonde village.

Christopher Chu Mbah and wife Eposi Kema have been accused of assaulting their landlady one Grace Enih and her daughter Geraldine Nim and caused them inability to walk for 28 and 30 days respectively. The two accused pleaded not guilty to the charge.

The Court heard that on the 22 day of December 2002, Mme Grace was in her house with her husband and their youngest daughter Clovis. A while later, her daughter called and informed her that Christopher was connecting an electricity cable from the neighbour. Quickly she got out of the house to stop Christopher from proceeding. Before she could utter a word, Christopher sent her a warning that if she (Mme Grace) dares, draw closer to him, he will beat her up. Mme Grace said before she realized it, Christopher had punched her right eye causing her to bleed. She shouted for help and her husband came out to intervene but Christopher insisted on connecting the cable.

Mme Grace told the Court that when her daughter Clovis tried to question why Christopher was beating her mother, Eposi came out of her room with a kitchen knife and threatened to stab Clovis if she dares open her mouth again. Geraldine who had just come in could not stand the ordeal and opted for a slash hammer but unfortunately Christopher and Eposi were stronger than her. They simply dragged her to their room where Eposi got her well beaten.

On seeing the seriousness of her bleeding, Mme Grace rushed to the hospital were she was attended to and given 28 days bed rest.

As if that was not enough, two days later, Eposi and her husband attacked Geraldine and tortured her very well for refusing them to tie a laundry rope through her (Geraldine) window as it would block the way to the toilet.

In her evidence Geraldine told the court that Eposi jumped over her and bit-off her right jaw following a brief altercation over the positioning of the laundry rope. Geraldine told the court that she immediately rushed to the hospital for medical attention after which she was given 30 days bed rest.

Mokindi village is bandits bee-hive

By Morara & Chipo

Mokindi village in Limbe Sub-Division has been described as the bee-hive for armed bandits in the area.

This is as a result of the high degree of crime wave as armed bandits have continuously terrorized the village in recent times.

The traditional ruler of the area Chief Ekane Alami, in a welcome address presented to the Divisional Officer during his maiden tour of the Sub-Division said that the high crime wave in the area has been aggravated further by the absence of streetlights.

Chief Ekane, however, commended government for the Limbe port to be built soon, the Limbe shipyard project already opened in Limbola and also the arrival of AES-Sonel project. He said with all these innovations he strongly believes that the youths will have substantial employment to support their parents.

Responding, the Divisional Officer called on the villagers to come out massively for the registration of voters in order to participate fully in the forth-coming presidential elections in order to attract development.

He further called on them to respect constituted authority by collaborating with traditional rulers who are auxillaries to government during community work amongst other development activities

Medallists should be exemplary in character, says Gov. Mbonda

By Marok Njiwaji

The Governor of the South West province, Thomas Ejake Mbonda, has called on all medal recipients to be exemplary in society and in the institution they serve. The Governor made this statement last May 11 in Limbe during the 8th ceremony for the award of labour medals to SONARA workers at the SONARA omnisport stadium-Bota.

Governor Ejake Mbonda also called on the medallists to espouse a collaboration spirit among themselves, adding that such spirit "inspires team spirit necessary for the survival of any establishment."

Mr Governor did not forget to register appreciation on the fact that the General Manager of SONARA, Mr Charles Metouck had organised the medal award ceremony for the workers.

Thomas Ejake Mbonda disclosed that the occasion was in line with the government policy of encouraging hard work, self-less dedication, among others. "Such qualities are what makes any establishment function well," said he.

He concluded by congratulating the staff and management for the pence that reigns supreme in the company.

On his part the Staff Representative, of SONARA, Divine Ebong Rede Epiekese, called for a moment of silence in respect of the fallen colleagues of the company, especially the former General Manager, Bernard Eding.

According to him, the refinery is working at its highest optimum and under the General Manager, Charles Metouck. Moreover, he extended heart-felt gratitude to those who gave special support to the refinery, adding that the success of SONARA today is the honour of the management. He added that the company has contributed immensely in the South West Province by offering assistance to Non Governmental Organisations (NGOs).

Meanwhile the General Manager of SONARA, Charles Metouck on his part revealed that the management of SONARA has always made it a point of duty to pay allegiance to its personnel and to award medals to them.

While congratulating everyone, he made special reference to those who will be crowned with gold medals. He stipulated that the majority of personnel in this group, if not all of them, are the trial-blazes of SONARA, who pressed the first button for the production of the company.

"Note that the necessary competitive spirit in our company to face the growing markets does not only require a technical and technological mastery in our case, but a more and more qualified, devoted, assiduous and competent personnel who will also be the soul of honesty."

Charles Metouck intimated that medallists should not rest on their laurels, rather, they should serve as examples in order to contribute more than before for the vision of the company. He also called on them to awaken their professional consciousness and carry on the spirit of togetherness "for a competitive SONARA and succinctly, a SONARA that wins."

He concluded by calling on the personnel of the refinery to meditate on the words of the wise man, Voltaire:

"To work is the only way to render life bearable."

In all, 152 medals of excellence were later awarded to workers of SONARA: 54 gold, 44 silver gilt and 54 silver.

Monday June 21, 2004

PAGE 2 *The* **POST** No. 0573 MONDAY, MAY 31, 2004

Monday Edition **NEWS**

Ndian SDO Disrupts Celebration Of World Artists' Day

George Ng[...]ne, SW Delegate of Culture

BY WALTER WILSON NANA

DANIEL Panjounou, Senior Divisional Of ficer, SDO, of Ndian ivision, May 26, ordered olice and gendarmes to dis- erse a crowd of traditional d choral groups, which had athered at the Ekondo Titi ommunity Field to com- emorate this year's World tists' Day.

Some 15 artists and sev- l traditional and choral oups from the Southwest ovince were in Ekondo i that day, at the invita- n of the Southwest Pro- icial Delegation of Cul- e, George Ngwane.

The Post gathered that en the SDO arrived at the mmunity Field, he ordered the police and the gendarmes to disperse the huge crowd that had been looking forward to a live musical concert from the Southwest artists.

The traditional and choral groups had earlier performed to the delight of the audience.

Emmanuel Eta, a.k.a Eta Unique, a Southwest-based artist, said, "We took off on a good note ... but things turned sour with the arrival of the SDO in Ekondo Titi at 6.00 pm. Rather than join us in the commemoration, he instead ordered the police and gendarmes to disperse the crowd."

Eta said the artists did not perform: "The crowd became disgruntled and dissatisfied with the unexpected reaction from the SDO."

Saying he saw sabotage in the SDO's action, Eta stated, "It tells you that he is culturally empty. Rather than working hand-in-glove with the Southwest Delegation of Culture, he instead brought disorder and disgrace, not only to the administration of the Province, but to Cameroon as a whole. I do not understand what must have happened with SDO."

Another Southwest-based singer, Elchic Echondong aka Amumba, said; "I am shocked with the reactions we had from the SDO on a special day and occasion like the World Day of Artists. After all the preparations and risks taken to get to Ekondo Titi, we did not perform at the 11th hour, due to the SDO's action.

"From what I gathered from the enthusiastic crowd that came to cheer us ..., the SDO ordered the gendarmes to forestall any performance by artists who have come from other parts of the Southwest Province. It is reported that he said we have come to disturb. Personally, I did not hear on the radio that the SDO had something to do in Ekondo Titi."

Ngwane, Delegate of Culture for the Southwest Province, assesses the problem: "Apparently, we had problems of power failure and poor weather. The other embarrassing and political angle was that the highest authority in Ndian Division gave an impression that I came to steal the crowd from him. He seemingly had his own message to pass across as concerns the upcoming election. I thought that we are all serving the same nation, and that if we had such a crowd, it was only normal for us to exploit it, and put our messages across. It will be fair for him to change methods in order to meet up with some of the problems that the people have in regard to the political set-up."

Asked if there might have been some administrative incoherence, Ngwane replied, "I took all my dispositions to be in Ekondo Titi in terms of presenting my programme to the Governor of the Southwest, informing the SDO of Ndian and drawing the necessary media attention. It has nothing to do with administrative incoherence, but more with character."

Ngwane, however, observed that: "I would not call it sabotage as it were. I think it is some misunderstanding about the role culture has. It seems the political insensitivity people are getting into, and the voter apathy is getting high now. However, we are bound to work together as administrators and to talk to the same audience. It was rather unfortunate that the SDO could not muster the crowd that turned out. I was not physically present at the time he came. I do not know exactly how the event was handled."

Attempts to get the Ndian SDO's comment before press time, failed.

Meantime, Ngwane, like the artists, has promised to make things bigger, come June 21, for the World Music Day commemoration, slated for Tombel, Kupe-Muanenguba, for the Southwest Province.

Fru Ndi Exhorts Bafuts To Pay Taxes

BY CHRIS MBUNWE

UNLIKE in 1992, when the opposition Social Democratic Front, SDF called for civil disobedience, the party now preaches against tax evasion.

That is why at the inauguration of a new market by the Bafut Rural Council, on May 25, the SDF National Chairman, Ni John Fru Ndi, urged the people of Bafut to pay market tolls to enable the Council repay its debt with FEICOM.

Addressing himself to the Director of FEICOM, His Royal Highness, Gerald Emmanuel Ondong Ndong, Fru Ndi requested for more market stalls.

"If you take into consideration the over 70,000 people of Bafut, you will understand that the 71 stalls are inadequate, that is to say 1000 people to one stall."

Also speaking at the occasion, the FEICOM boss said development has no political colouration and as such the Bafut people should be grateful to the government and use the new market to fight poverty.

The Mayor of Bafut, Henry Akoso Neba, said when the Bafut Rural Council applied for a loan from FEICOM to construct 100 market stalls at the cost of FCFA 59.272.205, "there was no Value Added Tax, VAT, in our tax system. By the time the loan was granted, VAT chopped part of it and the Council was forced to reduce the number of stalls to 71 with a total cost of FCFA 67.615.800 million."

Of this amount, the Council contributed FCFA 13.523.160 million and FEICOM's loans stood at FCFA 36.061.760 to be paid in four annual installments by the Bafut Rural Council.

The Fon of Bafut, HRH Abumbi II, while presenting some artefacts to HRH Ondong Ndong, said the new market will relieve the Bafut people from remnants of colonial relics constructed by the Germans in 1947.

Professor Aletum Tabuwe, revealed that FEICOM's Director told him in private that his institution will finance the Bafut Water Project at the cost of FCFA 40 million.

"As my classmate, I am very confident he is going to realise this project," Tabuwe said.

NEO President Campaigned For CPDM At 2002 Twin Elections'

Headteacher Sacked For Swindling Exams Fees

BY MIRABEL AZANGRH

PAGE 10

The Post No. 0580 FRIDAY, JUNE 25, 2004

Weekender

Collector's Diary

Saturday 5 - The first time good news was startling: that good news was news at all, was when news reached us that Paul Biya, His Excellency, the President of the Republic of Cameroon, had died somewhere in Europe. Those who had always silently wished him death built bon fires, bought prodigious litres of wines, whisky and lager and settled down for a long riotous vigil. For those who ride on Biya's back for a living, it was a black day. They shut themselves inside their houses, turned off the lights and spent the rest of the night crying themselves blind. And for those whom Biya had bored to near death or stopped from eating the national cake, sighed with relief at the timely departure of the ogre. Little did they, we, in fact, know that in a matter of days we would be treated to a walking corpse, a zombie, an apparition of Biya... hm.

As I said, we gathered in our favourite bar and drank ourselves blind. In the middle of the night, one of us, noted for his dry humour, suddenly slammed his bottle on the table, miraculously it did not shatter. He twisted his mouth into a most grotesque shape, clasped his head in his hands and yelled: "*shoo*, Paul Biya! *Chei! Weei!* Did you have to die now? *Weh! Ooooh!!* He sniffed. He whimpered. He banged the tabletop. We thought it was funny and exploded into laughter. The man rose on his feet, jaws set, lips twitching nervously, eyes hot and reddened, popping out of his head, a humourless sneer twinkling in them; the entire face craggy, bitter. He scowled at us sounding curiously as if he wanted to fortify a spurious act.

"What is so funny? Scoundrels."

We shut up our mouths. If it wasn't for a smile that vanished swiftly from the corner of his mouth, we might have believed that the man was rightly aggrieved by Biya's death.

"Bullshit!" he muttered under his breath and sat down. This time we burst into such rapturous laughter that made our ribs ache and left us giddy.

Monday 7 – I was rummaging through my papers, drawers, books, pockets and so on for a telephone number I had misplaced, when I saw the flap of a paper packet lying on the floor, under the bedroom table. I had to get down on my knees to reach it. I couldn't remember if I ever kept such a piece of cardboard with a phone number on it. All the same, I felt better since I had to make this call. I dialled the number which started with 776... A deep husky male voice rumbled from the other end.

"Yes, hullo, Patience," it said, putting in a good quantity of erotic softness in the word Patience. I cocked my ear and pressed the phone harder on it.

"Hullo, Patience, *is* that you, Patience? Talk to me darling..." I switched off the phone. I sat on the bed and felt hot beads of sweat popping on my forehead. Then I heard my heart beating hard and fast in my chest: thump, thump, thump. I put the piece of card in my wallet and left quietly.

Wednesday 9 – I was in a cab, my car was in a *laverie*, and the news cast in French was on air... *le chef de l'etat... reviendra au jour d'hui... il ... a l'aeroport de Nsimalen a 16 heures...*

Damn it!

"Did they say Biya is coming back today?" I flung the question to the driver.

"Yes," the driver said and shifted into low gear.

"When Biya died this morning?" said a man sitting to my right. He leaned back in the seat with a certain air of certainty and looked out the window.

"But the radio has just announced that he is landing this afternoon," I said, glancing at the man.

"Yes," said the driver, looking backwards at the man to my right. He fixed his gaze outside at the trees whizzing past and said flatly:

"Biya died this morning," and waved his hand in the air.

"Who told you?" I asked.

"I was in town this morning. A friend told me," the man said, still gazing outside.

"And how did the man know?" I pressed.

"Hm... well... but Biya is dead anyway." That is when he looked at me and smiled faintly. I suppose he was expecting approval from me. But although I did want to believe that Biya was alive, I chuckled at the man's insistence.

Friday 11 – I can't recall clearly when I went for this party, but I remember it was something like ASJUB, Association of Journalist Students of UB, something like that. I don't know. But I remember very well how we blew the place up - girls! Buttocks of all sizes and shapes, dozens of hairstyles, perfumes, smells; cheap ones and all. Girls!

About 2:00 am - The warm up was violent - the girl I had never before collected, a wild cat, she defended herself with nails and elbows and teeth. Then she felt tired and I saw she loved it. When I scooped her in my arms and flung her on the bed, I kissed her and the bed began to creak.

The Collector

Stars Infos

World Music Day 2004:

Pomp, Fanfare In Tombel

BY WALTER WILSON NANA

Culture Delegate (second from left) and guests watching a dance group performing on World Music Day in Tombel

SUNDAY, June 20, it was all joy, ambiance and colourful at the Tombel Council Hall. The issue was a live performance of artists based in the Southwest Province. They were party to the World Music Day commemoration, June 21. The event came to fruition, thanks to the Southwest Provincial Delegation of Culture and the Tombel Rural Council.

More than 10 traditional and choral groups from the Tombel municipality converged at the esplanade of the Tombel Council to be part of the show. Artists based in the Southwest Province came in their numbers. These included; Lawrence Esong, Elchic Echendong, aka Anumba, Njoume Loko, Lama Lobe, Jojo Mussenja, Mary Mandi, Tchaya Stoppeur, Bright Muabe, Esele Bijou, Ngole Ebenzu, Elone Emougene, Ngeme Ngalame, Ernest Alobwede, Nelson Ngando, Martin Lekunze, Divine Njanwa, Valentine Fotabe and James Ayuk.

These men and women of show business were up to the task. They showcased their artistic savvy. In communion with the large audience turnout, applause and applause followed. The rhythms blared the air. And the enthusiastic crowd would not go home. Even at 2:00 a.m. After all, it is not everyday that live music is heard in Tombel. Even the Mayor of Tombel Rural Council, Nhon Dr. Ntoko Mekolle Epie, could not resist singing alongside Reggae Boy Bob Aboki, from Kumba.

WHEN the curtains were drawn, the Tombel denizens, the administrative authorities like the artists were in unison, happy and appreciative. Bright Muabe said: "I am grateful to have been part of the World Music Day, 2004. It came and met me in Tombel. I play high-life *makossa* and *ngone* (a Bakossi rhythm)."

Roland Esokane, choreographer, was very pleased; "I am happy. I have once tried my hands in music. I love music naturally. I will welcome the Delegation of Culture, Southwest, when they come next."

Another artist, Ngome Ngalame, appreciated the initiative of the Southwest Provincial Delegation of Culture.

"I think it is a very good initiative. These things happen in Buea, Limbe, Kumba, and sometimes the poor road network and communication hinder us to participate out there. So, it becomes difficult to discover the talents buried here in Tombel. It is an opportunity for some of us and younger people to be inspired and pushed ahead. They should know that music and culture are things that sell. It could bring in a lot of money."

A happy Mayor, Dr. Ntoko was, had this reaction: "I am a very happy Mayor. It is 2:00 a.m and we are still here. It tells you that we are in support of the World Music Day 2004 in Tombel. We support the activities of the Ministry of Culture. It is very thrilling. 2004 is just the tip of the iceberg. 2005, we shall be better prepared and make it real big."

An elated Simon Becke, Inspector of Primary and Nursery Education, Tombel, said; "It has been wonderful. For the first time, we are grateful. We are delighted to have live music in Tombel. It has been a total success. It has been super."

On her part, Mrs. Ekome, Financial Secretary, KUMUACULA, Tombel, holds that it is a dream come true. "I am very glad to have seen some of the musicians live. I had seen them only on television. For a long time we have not achieved such a goal in Tombel. We are very happy to see it for the first time. Besides the World Music Day, I will love that the authorities and the people of Tombel invite the artists some other time, so that we enjoy in unison."

According to the Southwest Provincial Delegate of Culture, George Ngwane, the International Music Day in his Province came to reality, thanks to the prop from SONARA, KUMUACULA, Tombel, Mr. Rufus Mbong and Dr. Eneme Andrew.

Dear Editor,

I did Not Regret Becoming A Priest

Your reporter who covered my jubilee celebration in Buea got facts wrong. Her statement was: "He said he regretted several times why he decided to join the priesthood." (*The Post* No. 0579 Monday June 21, 2004, P.6)

The statement itself contradicts what is contained in the rest of the article. I said emphatically that if I were asked to choose again, I would remain a priest forever.

Sincerely yours,
Fr. Moses Tazoh

Editor's Note:
We deeply regret the error!

www.thepostnewspaper.org

Let me return to the newspaper clipping with the headline "Ndian SDO Disrupts Celebration of World Artists' Day" to give further insight. My staff and I arrived at Ekondo Titi on May 25th 2004 and were treated to a hectic dinner party by the Bakossi community in the premises of my parents-in-law Chief and Mrs Panje. Part of the reason I choose Ekondo Titi to celebrate the World Artist Day was because I wanted to break away from celebrations of cultural activities centred only in the metropolis especially in Buea to move them to the periphery where talents were hidden and where creativity was eclipsed under inaccessible roads and lack of promotion. The other reason was that I needed to make my first cultural outreach tour to a place I was familiar with and Ekondo Titi and by extension Ndian division symbolized many metaphors and narratives in my life. I did my Primary School at Government Primary School Lobe in the mid-70s. I taught in Government High School Mundemba from 1986-1991. I got married and had my first two children in Mundemba in 1987-1990. I carried out my first civil strike with twenty-two other teachers on 12th December 1988 in Mundemba protesting against PAMOL Company for making the roads inaccessible to our students. I was detained for two weeks in the Brigade Mixte Mobile in Ekondo Titi for writing an article on our lopsided bilingual policy in March 1990. I published my first book "The Mungo Bridge" in September 1990 in Mundemba. So early the following morning of May 26th I met Chief Dr. Esoh Itor (Chief of Ekondo Titi and the then Mayor of Ekondo Titi Council) and late Chief Ngomo Elambo (President of Ekondo Titi Cultural Association) as our contact persons on the ground to find out about the preparations for the World Artists' day which essentially was composed of choral jamboree by choir groups in Ekondo Titi and live band performance from Buea. I knew Chief Itor's meticulous sense of organisation as he was my teacher in Government Primary School Lobe in the mid-70s. Apart from being my classroom teacher, Chief was a Sports and Music Teacher. There was no choral competition in the area among schools without our school coming first. His songs especially in the local dialect charmed the jury and the audience. My father who was then the Schools Manager for the Division used to stop over in our Primary School to teach us songs mainly in English but the real male nightingale of the area was Teacher Itor. So when he assured me that all was set for the World Artist Day I was relaxed. But what kept Chief Itor, Chief Ngomo Elambo and my staff on our toes on that May 26th 2004 was the time the event would take off at the ceremony square in Ekondo Titi. We had a problem with the time schedule because my arrival at Ekondo Titi coincided with the official tour of the then Senior Divisional Officer (S.D.O) of Ndian Division. The S.D.O was on a tour to sensitise the Ndian population on voter registration against rising voter apathy. His stop over at Ekondo Titi was on the same day I had programmed the cultural event and we needed to wait for him to commission the event and then pass on his message on voter registration towards the Presidential elections of October 2004. After a long wait, after trying to reach the S.D.O's delegation by phone in vain and seeing how restive the choristers were, Chief Itor and I decided to begin the World Artist Day as late as 4 pm. I have never witnessed such a rainbow display of costumes and a diversity of voices from cultural groups like I did in Ekondo Titi. The ceremonial ground which coincidentally was facing the very Brigade Mixte Mobile in which was detained in 1990 was alive with music renting the air as choral groups outperformed each other in indigenous songs and artistic choreography. More than 15 choral groups filed past the ceremonial ground leaving the population in total frenzy for at least two hours. Then at about 6 pm the live band from Buea made its entry into the ceremonial ground with the pomp and arrogance characteristic of musicians. And the band held its own, rendering songs the population got only from the radio and the musicians reaching out to the crowd for fellowship. By 9pm it started drizzling and I was forced to retire to my sleeping abode for a well-deserved night rest. I was awakened the following morning by Chief and Mrs Panje on a strange but sad note. After I retired from the choral and live band event, the S.D.O arrived at the ceremonial ground and tried to stop the event in order to brief the population on voter registration. Unfortunately for the S.D.O the population did not want politics to interfere with their creative ecstasy and so resorted to booing. Frustrated and bitter, the S.D.O tried to get the madding crowd to reason and then resorted to rain invectives on the visiting Provincial Delegate of Culture who dared to invade his territory and set up such a 'rude' and 'rowdy' crowd that prevented him from delivering a very important election message. Who he questioned was this Delegate who did not have the courtesy to inform him about his presence in his area of command? To be fair to the S.D.O I did not for three reasons stop at his office to signal my presence as it is required. First I thought that after informing the Governor of the province of my calendar of activities in the various divisions, it was the Governor to send messages through fax or telex to the authorities concerned. It was indeed both an oversight and administrative naivety on my part. Second, I arrived at Ekondo Titi on the eve of the event and even if I had plans to travel to Mundemba (the headquarters of Ndian Division), I would not have met the S.D.O who was at that moment in another village called Toko for his voter sensitization tour. Thirdly after trying in vain to get him on the phone, we assumed that he would just be too happy to meet with a readymade crowd for his political message especially as he arrived at Ekondo Titi at about 9.30pm when the town without my cultural event would have been asleep. He ranted and raved on my insubordination with threats to take up the matter to my Buea and Yaounde hierarchy. Whether he did I do not know but what I know is that this incident triggered my subsequent suspension and dismissal as Delegate. This Ekondo Titi incident would have been diplomatically managed if one was living under less high handed administration which by its logic and reckoning places control, command and intimidation above all else.

From March 10th 2004 to June 20th 2004, I had fulfilled my short term calendar of Activities as can be seen from this 1st Semester Report which was submitted to my hierarchy.

SOUTH WEST PROVINCIAL DELEGATION OF CULTURE BUEA

1ST SEMESTER REPORT 2003/2004

No	PERIOD	TYPE OF ACTIVITY	VENUE	OBSERVATION
1	March 10th 2004	Handing over to new Provincial Delegate George Ngwane	Buea Delegation	Presided over by DAG
2	March 16th 2004	Burial of Cameroonian Musician Sammy Mafany	Buea Likoko Membea	Colorful participation of 20 Artists from the S.W. (painters, musicians sculpture, writers) high-level delegation from MINCULT. Yaounde.
3	April 19th 2004	French German Cameroonian week	AFC Buea	The Provincial Delegate presented a speech at the opening Ceremony.
4	April 21st 2004	Meeting with Videogramme exploiters.	Tiko District office	Successful meeting but exploiters plead for drastic drop of Culture tax.
5	April 23rd 2004	**World Book Day**	Cameroon Cultural Center Buea	Book exhibition by 6 exhibitors, children's book parade with primary school pupils, panel discussion with 8 writers.
6	April 29th 2004	Meeting with videogramme exploiters	Limbe Chamber of Commerce	Successful meeting but exploiters plead for drastic drop of Culture of Tax.
7	April 30th 2004	Meeting with videogramme exploiters	Muyuka D.O.office	Successful meeting but exploiters plead for drastic drop of Culture of Tax.
8	May 4th 2004	Beginning of Provincial Tour in Meme Division	Kumba	Successful meeting with compilation of list of all Artists in Meme Division.
9	May 6th 2004	Meeting with Artists in Tombel for Kupe Mwanenguba	Tombel	Successful meeting with compilation of list of all Artists in Meme Division.
10	May 11th 2004	Meeting of Artists in Manyu division	Mamfe	Successful
11	May 13th 2004	**World Museum Day** Meeting of Artists in Lebialem division	Menji	Turn out of more than 30 sculptors for exhibition.
No	PERIOD	TYPE OF ACTIVITY	VENUE	OBSERVATION
12	May 26th 2004	**World Artist Day** Meeting of Artists in Ndian division	Ekondo titi	Turn out of more than 25 dance groups and 15 musicians. Interruption by S.D.O. Ndian
13	May 28th 2004	Meeting of Artists of Fako division in Tiko	Tiko	Compilation of names of Artists in Tiko.
14	June 15th 2004	Meeting of Artist of Fako division in Buea	Buea	Successful
15	June 20th 2004	**Fête de la Musique**	Tombel	Traditional dances, choir, 15 musicians

On the 8th June 2004, I received the following letter in my office from the Governor's Office.

REPUBLIQUE DU CAMEROUN
PAIX - TRAVAIL - PATRIE

PROVINCE DU SUD-OUEST

SERVICES DU GOUVERNEUR

Vos Ref :...........................
Your Ref :

Nos Ref :...........................
Our Ref :

REPUBLIC OF CAMEROON
PEACE - WORK - FATHERLAND

SOUTH WEST PROVINCE

GOVERNOR'S OFFICE

N° 578 /L/G/GSW.13/S.3/SG/CASC

Buea, the 07 JUIN 2004
le

The Governor of the South-West Province
Le Gouverneur de la Province du Sud-Ouest

Subject: LETTER OF OBSERVATION: DISLOYALTY AND UNPATRIOTIC ATTITUDE.

To: Mr. GEORGE NGWANE,
PROVINCIAL DELEGATE
FOR CULTURE,
SOUTH WEST PROVINCE
- BUEA -

My attention has been drawn to seditious and libellous articles written and made published by you in The Post Newspaper. The articles are:

- *Indigenous democratic visions in Africa*: The Post N° 0566 of Monday, May 3rd 2004, Page 8.
- *Pauperisation of Cameroonian Masses*: The Post N° 0570 of Monday, May 17th 2004, Page 8.
- *Beyond Presidentials 2004*: The Post N° 0573 of Monday, May 31st 2004, Page 8.

In the article, "*Indigenous Democratic Visions in Africa*", you have categorised H.E. Paul Biya as one of those political leaders in Cameroon who has personalised power, because since the creation of the C.P.D.M. in 1985, he has always presented himself as candidate for all Presidential Elections without going through C.P.D.M. party primaries. This you continue, in contrast to Mr. John Fru Ndi, who in 1997 went through primaries within the S.D.F. party as candidate for Presidential Elections.

Further, you examined political leadership in Cameroon since independence and you had this to say:

1) That H.E. Paul Biya dwells on philosophical and erudite rhetoric while Ahidjo dwelt on feasible and concrete projects.

2) That H.E. Paul Biya's leadership's style is by proxy and his diplomacy is that of distance and discretion while Ahidjo's leadership style was that of rapprochement and a diplomacy of proximity and presence.

<u>In the article "*Pauperisation of Cameroonian Masses*"</u>, you condemn the privatisation policy of the government and particularly that of the C.D.C. Further, you say Cameroon is crammed with wealth, yet the population is in misery, and this particularly as Cameroon is taken hostage by the IMF and Brethren Woods. You end this article noting that democracy in Cameroon without development is as useless as winning football trophies as we do in Cameroon without football stadia.

<u>In the article "*Beyond Presidential 2004*"</u>, you say since 1990, Cameroon's democratic process is like a journey without maps particularly as you read and echo Ntemfac Ofege's mind that "Mr. Biya, will always rig elections".

Whereas the preamble of the 1996 Constitution guarantees public liberty to all citizens, and whereas the 1990 Laws give the citizens the liberty to think, write and act freely within the armpits of the law, it is disturbing to note that a Provincial Delegate, should take pride in intoxicating and hoodwinking national and international opinion about the President of the Republic and the institutions he incarnates. This is why I interpret your actions as grossly disloyal and unpatriotic because you have not only failed to maintain the high degree of reserve you ought to, but you have equally betrayed the confidence the State has in you.

While seizing this opportunity to call you to order, let me also know within 24hrs upon the receipt of this letter of observation, why severe sanctions should not be meted against you for disloyalty, and unpatriotic attitudes against the institutions of the Republic.

THE GOVERNOR

REPUBLIQUE DU CAMEROUN / REPUBLIC OF CAMEROON / LE GOUVERNEUR / THE GOVERNOR / SOUTH WEST PROVINCE / PROVINCE DU SUD OUEST

Thomas Efake Mbonde
Administrateur Civil Principal

2

On 5th July 2004, I was invited to Yaounde by my Ministry to attend a workshop on immoveable cultural patrimony in Cameroon. I was in the company of other Provincial Delegates for close to 3 days which ended with the following assignment- I was assigned to make an inventory of the historical monuments and sites of the South West Province.

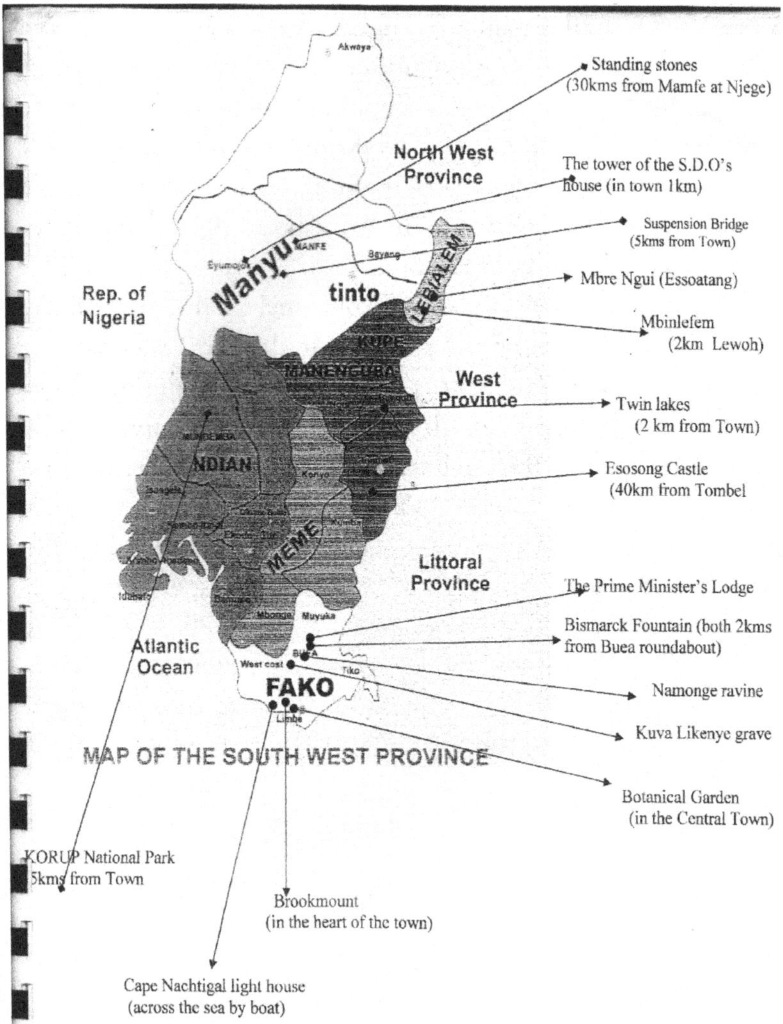

MAP indicating KEY Sites and Monuments in the Province

However on the second day of the workshop I was called on phone by Mr Nkong Makoge (then Provincial Delegate of Communication for South West) to the effect that a fax had just been sent to my office suspending me as Delegate. Nkong advised me to meet my Minister Leopold Oyono or his Secretary General who was actually running the Ministry to explain my story. Even though I knew it was a fait accompli, I met the Secretary General who indicted me on my political adrenalin and the disappointment and ingratitude I had shown the Prime Minister who endorsed my appointment as Delegate. The Secretary General advised me to go prepare my file because I was going to be arraigned before the Discipline Council of the Public Service. I went back to the workshop and broke the news to my colleagues and left back for Buea.

On 8th July 2004 even without seeing the fax of my suspension, I convened my staff and told them I was packing out of the office. I handed the keys of my office and the car to my interim Mr Roger Lita. It was at this moment that I got a phone call from the Cultural and Social Adviser in the Governor's Office, Reverend Victor Ayuk. He gleefully and with all the sarcasm of a patriotic conqueror handed to me in the presence of Madam Meg Agbor this letter of Suspension.

REPUBLIQUE DU CAMEROUN
Paix-Travail-Patrie
MINISTERE DE LA CULTURE

REPUBLIC OF CAMEROON
Peace-Work-Fatherland
MINISTRY OF CULTURE

DECISION N° 004/09 /MINCULT DU
PORTANT SUSPENSION DE M. NGWANE Georges ESSAMBE
DE SES FONCTIONS

LE MINISTRE D'ETAT CHARGE DE LA CULTURE

Vu la Constitution,
Vu le Décret n° 97/205 du 07 décembre 1997 portant organisation du Gouvernement, modifié et complété par le décret n° 98/067 du 28 avril 1998 ;
Vu le décret n° 97/207 portant formation du Gouvernement et ses modificatifs subséquents ;
Vu le décret n° 98/003 du 08 janvier 1998 portant organisation du Ministère de la Culture ;
Vu le décret n°94-199 du 7 octobre 1994 portant Statut général de la Fonction publique de l'Etat ,
Vu l'arrêté n° 003 /MINCULT du 05 mars 2004 portant nomination des responsables au Ministère de la Culture ;
Vu l'urgence et les nécessités de services ;

DECIDE

Article 1er : Monsieur NGWANE Georges ESSAMBE, Délégué provincial de la Culture pour le Sud-Ouest, est pour compter de la date de signature de la présente décision suspendu de ses fonctions.

Article 2 : Monsieur LITA Roger, Chef de service provincial de la Cinématographie, assurera l'intérim du Délégué provincial de la Culture pour le Sud-Ouest pendant la durée de cette suspension.

Article 3 : La présente décision sera enregistrée, puis communiquée partout ou besoin sera.

Ampliations :
- SG/PM
- MINFOPRA
- GOUVERNEUR DE LA PROVINCE DU SUD-OUEST
- INTERESSE
- ARCHIVES

Fait à Yaoundé, le [illegible]6 JUIL. 2004

Ferdinand Leopold OYONO

My last part of the article "Cameroon's Democratic Process-Vision 2020" had appeared in the Post newspaper of Monday June 28, 2004. Here is the complete article that provoked the letter of Observation and subsequently the Letter of Suspension.

Cameroon's Democratic Process: Vision 2020

The underlying assumption of this essay is that multipartyism has failed in Cameroon not because multipartyism has proven to be an ill-adapted political model in most of Africa but because the political elite in Cameroon have been unable to provide a vision of a future for Cameroonians and a realistic strategy for achieving it. The essay therefore calls on Cameroonians to see beyond Presidential elections 2004 and to ponder over the question: 'What will Cameroon look like in the year 2020?'

Introduction

It is 2004; Cameroon is in the heat of another multiparty election fever. Since the elections are presidential, the stakes are high and the expectations even higher. Leaders of thought and presidential hopefuls are raising their apocalyptic voices above the din of disillusionment just like it happened in 1992 and in 1997. Since Multipartyism got reintroduced in Cameroon in 1990, Cameroonians have learnt to make do with a presumptuous yet ubiquitous incumbent and an ambitious yet fragmented opposition.

Democratic content

For more than a decade, the goals of multiparty democracy still elude the masses and within the present political context of unbridled demagogy, multiparty may remain a façade and charade, promising much but delivering little. Many reasons have been advanced for the dismal performance of neo-liberal democracy in Cameroon but let us dwell on just a few.

Lack of democratic will

Cameroon's leadership yielded to democratic pressures (both internal and external) in the early 1990s more out of convenience than of conviction. In his political book *Communal Liberalism*, the incumbent President, Paul Biya, had manifested his apprehension for multipartyism as he wrote: 'A new generation in Africa is within the range of a new vision of the best future Africa is yet to see.' Jonathan N. Moyo, Minister of Information, Zimbabwe. The present phase of the history of Cameroon does not permit the institution of a multiparty system. Our Party (Cameroon People's Democratic Movement–CPDM) is therefore responsible for the reduction of the existing ethno-cultural divisions in order to promote national integration… (Biya 1987: 127). Hardly had Paul Biya, who took power as President in 1982 from Amadou Ahidjo, settled down to experiment his political thought than the 6 April 1984 aborted military coup jostled his grip on power and the 26 May 1990 launching of another political party (Social Democratic Front – SDF) defied his one party ideology. From May–November 1990, opponents of multiparty politics marched the streets of Cameroon calling those who had dared to upset the apple's cart 'merchants of illusions' and 'enemies of national unity'. This did not stem the tide of internal pressure. As for external forces the then French President François Mitterrand believed to have facilitated Biya's accession to power, made a speech at La Baule (France) in the direction that African countries should henceforth 'expand their democratic spaces.' Arguably because of Cameroon's legendary servitude to France, the Biya leadership reneged on its initial ideology of one party rule. At the same time the international community was waving the 'stick and carrot' bait to African countries reluctant to swallow multiparty democracy. Prominent among them was the then British Foreign Secretary Douglas Hurd who said 'those countries tending towards pluralism, public accountability, respect for human rights, and market principles, should be encouraged.

But governments which persist with repressive policies... should not expect us to support their folly with the scarce resources which could be better used elsewhere' (*Africa Confidential:* 1991).

With both internal and external pressures on Paul Biya, but without any concrete rules on the exigencies of multiparty politics, without a change of the monolithic constitution, without a defined role of the opposition, without a clear cut line between the party and state and without any referendum, he (Biya) promulgated into law on 19 December 1990, the reintroduction of multiparty democracy in Cameroon (Ngwane 1996: 175).

Lack of democratic transition

Patrick Quantrin highlighted several features of the democratisation processes in Africa for over a decade as non-transition, transitions without change, authoritarian rehabilitation and fragile transitions (cited in *CODESRIA Bulletin*, 2002) Cameroon was one of the countries that embarked on a non-transition democracy. Either oblivious of or bankrupt in other political models, Cameroon trigger-happily discarded the 'devil' of the one party system to embrace the 'god' of multipartyism. But unlike other African countries, like Benin (1990), Mali (1991), then Zaire (1991) and South Africa (1994) that planned a transition, the leadership of Cameroon resisted any form of democratic transition. Such a context only encouraged the emergence of a new elite in the political arena, next to the old ones who switched over, for the occasion, to the virtues of political pluralism (Tidjani Alou 2002: 28). The setting up of Constitutional Conferences, Sovereign National Conferences and Truth and Reconciliation Commissions as modes of transition was meant to provide new political and economic paradigms suited to the demands of pluralism. As discussion forums, transition modes served as the balm of national reconciliation and catharsis as well as avenues to put in place reforms and structures that would change the quality of lives of the masses. When President Paul Biya therefore declared on 27 June 1991 at the National Assembly that 'Je l'ai dit et je le maintiens, la conférence nationale est sans objet pour le Cameroun' (I insist that a national conference is baseless in Cameroon). Cameroonians were stunned into both rage and revolt. Biya's refusal to yield to popular demand for a national conference was partly due to the opposition parties' misconception of the purpose of such a conference–their perception was not one of overhauling the obsolete monolithic apparatus but one of impeaching and eventually stripping Biya of legitimate power. Cameroonians therefore missed a rare opportunity to reassess the gains of independence and to examine the expectations of a democratic renewal. Instead, Biya offered Cameroonians a Tripartite Conference consisting of the ruling party, the opposition and the civil society. This conference that was held from 30 October –18 November 1991 proved to be futile as national aspirations became mortgaged on the altar of parochialism. The main weakness of this conference was the quasi-obsessional temptations of the ruling party, which wanted rules and results for its prime benefit alone.

Lack of democratic vision

When the wind of change blew in Africa in the late 1980s and early 1990s most countries made the error of aping neo-liberal democracy as if no other innovative and home-grown democratic choices existed. It was as if 'greater democracy' automatically meant multipartyism and multipartyism was seen to be succeeding only if elections were free or fair. Whatever the reason for the emphasis on multiparty election it is misleading and threatening to the process of democratisation in Africa because it trivialises democracy (Ake 2000: 150). The Cameroonian experience proves that while the ruling party sees multiparty election as a source of prebend, the opposition supports it as a strategy of power. Each one wants to sustain or inherit the system not necessarily to change it. The over fourteen years of Cameroonian democracy is arguably all about voting without choosing. Despite these multiparty years, most Cameroonians have had little reason to believe that they are anything other than pawns in a game of chess played by the power elite. The latter set their agendas for the masses, use them (masses) to serve their ends and abandon them to the misery and ignorance to which they are accustomed (Nyamnjoh 2002). By reducing democracy to a historical practice of election and the peddling of compensatory development advantages to the voter, multipartyism only seeks to hold the ordinary citizen in perpetual captivity. To be sure this capture may be sweetened by allurements and material inducements, which underline the contempt and devalorisation of the voter (Ake 2000: 170). Indeed, with human development now being replaced with the triumph of peace, the success of Cameroon's multiparty experience lies only in counting up the number of permitted parties as in the medieval manner of counting up the number of angels who can stand on the point of a pin (Davidson 1991). Peace is a means to an end; the ultimate end being development. And so Cameroonians sometimes look back with nostalgia at the Amadou Ahidjo authoritarian years of one party rule, when they enjoyed economic prosperity. According to Milton Krieger, Cameroonians sustained steady, even (with petroleum's help) buoyant growth in the economy, and sufficient patterns of opportunity in the patronage distribution of their domestic proceeds. There was enough for many Cameroonians to aspire to, if not to attain (Krieger 1994: 607). From all indications, the quest for greater democracy in the 1990s in Cameroon was predicated on greater participation in decision- making, greater devolution of power to the regions, greater focus on the Anglophone problem, greater ownership by the population of its natural resources and assets of Independence, greater economic empowerment and greater, fairer and more equal opportunities for any Cameroonian to contest and win any elective position. Unfortunately, Cameroon like most African countries embraced multipartyism not as a vista of social democracy but as a reversal of fortunes from the dominant ruling party (CPDM) to the sharing of sources of prebends and centres of power to party coalitions in proportion to their political or vocal weight. Lest we forget, Africa is not in short supply of indigenous democratic visions, hence the no-party system in Uganda, the consensual democracy in Swaziland and the new found consociational democracy in Rwanda. Cameroon itself is not in short supply of state persons who can provide a democratic vision that has an organic socio-historical link with the dynamics of its social formations. The problem is that innovative rather than orthodox ideologies are easily met with institutional blockages even from the political parties themselves like Mila Assoute's 'White book' in the CPDM party or the Article 8.2 subversion act in the SDF. The repercussions of the absence of a democratic will, democratic transition and democratic vision on Cameroon's political, social and economic landscapes are as many as they are complex, but let us spell out just a few.

Personalisation of power

Cameroon's present Parliament (2004) is made up of five parties. The CPDM, SDF, Cameroon Democratic Union (CDU), National Union for Democracy and Progress (NUDP) and the Union des Populations du Cameroun (UPC). The founders of these political parties have remained leaders of their parties since their creation (for the CPDM since 1985 and the rest since 1990). The founders/ leaders have presented themselves as candidates for all presidential elections without first submitting themselves to primary elections within their respective parties. Apart from the SDF that in 1997 was obliged to stage-manage primary elections between the incumbent leader Ni John Fru Ndi and the little-known and Paris-based Chretien Tabetsing, the other parties have acted as if their leaders, Paul Biya (CPDM), Ndam Njoya (CDU), Bello Bouba (NUDP), and Augustine Kodock (UPC) were 'les candidates naturels' and 'Présidents à vie de leur parti' (life presidents of their parties). The lesson one can draw from this is that there is no political culture of alternatives and debate in Cameroon since each founder/ leader has positioned himself to the point of confiscating party powers (Biombi 2001: 5). This tenacity syndrome characteristic of African heads of state does not augur well with those who wish to steer the state of affairs in a new dispensation. Probably the worst form of power confiscation is in Cameroon's state corporations. Some of the barons of these corporations have overstayed their grip on these corporations that they act as if they had no one to render account to. As auditing is a rare feat in Cameroon, the barons parade with state wealth, distribute it in *CODESRIA Bulletin,* Nos 3 & 4, 2004 Page 22 fake philanthropy until the corporations are brought to ruin or to privatisation. It was as if Cameroon was an empire with parastatals looking like personal kingdoms. This phenomenon of patrimonial and personalised management of public affairs now runs through every facet of the Cameroonian bureaucracy. No one sees his/her office as a civil/state property for which service has to be granted without favours; tribalism, nepotism, laxity and egoism are now at loggerheads with nationalism and patriotism. Public and even the private sectors have openly become racketeering spaces; the law officer on the road, the teacher in school, the nurse in the hospital, the magistrate in court and the typist in the secretariat. Everyone is master and the only boss is God. Civil servants are using the cloak of party loyalty to kill the efficiency of the public service. It must be for this reason that Paul Biya's address to the nation on 31st December 2003 focused on the word 'inertia'. He decried the public service which is plagued by deplorable laissez-faire, laxity and lack of good citizenship. But while the ordinary citizen is an accomplice to this crime, he or she is only drawing inspiration from his/her almighty bosses.

Embourgeoisement of the state

For the most part, the political atrophy and economic malaise Cameroon is facing can be blamed on its political elite. The political elite have failed to squarely and frankly address and redress the problems in Cameroon preferring instead to safeguard their privileges and sinecures. Since President Biya has adopted the seminarist approach of leadership (dwelling on philosophical and abstract rhetoric) unlike Ahidjo's pragmatic approach (dwelling on feasible and concrete projects), since Biya has dwelt on a leadership by proxy with a routine agenda, unlike Ahidjo's leadership by rapprochement with a reform agenda, since Biya's diplomacy is one of distance and discretion, unlike Ahidjo's diplomacy of proximity and presence, the elite in Cameroon have arrogated to themselves the wisdom to interpret every gesture and intention of the President. It is this political elite, which occupy public space; garbed in Biya's effigy, they tell the masses of Biya's messianic achievements and drum support for his eternity in power. They do this knowing that their own survival depends largely on their loyalty to the man and not to the nation or the institutions. It is not about supporting the system wholeheartedly, it is about the benefits that accrue from this hypocrisy. In the end the building of nationhood has been sacrificed on the altar of self-aggrandisement and personality cult. Instead of the political elite being the people's earphone they have become the president's megaphone; instead of the political elite being role models, they alienate citizens and act in their own corporate interest, erecting new ascriptive barriers that limit positive contributions to national life and development (Nsamenang 1992: 117). Until the state of Cameroon recognises that vocal party militancy is not always tantamount to inordinate patriotism; until it recognises that the rent seeking behaviour of the elite has retarded the pace of shared citizenship and national concord, Cameroon's leadership shall never establish a true partnership with a greater number of its human resources–the masses, and democracy is also about numbers. No democracy is as dangerous as one that puts premium on people (elite) with a high consumption capacity over a people (masses) with a high productive potential. Indeed if the democracy of the elite prevails, Africa would have democratised in form but not in content, and in a way that is largely irrelevant to its social realities (Ake 2000: 192).

Pauperisation of the masses

Despite the fact that Cameroon has one of the best endowed primary commodity economies in sub-Saharan Africa, its population remains among the least in human development. In 1993, government slashed civil servants' salaries by 70 per cent and in 1994 the CFA franc was devalued by 50 per cent. This, according to Clovis Atatah, considerably weakened the buying power of Cameroonians thus jeopardising the chances of a consumer-led economic growth (Atatah 2003: 11). This economic crisis has been compounded by the draconian structural adjustment measures of the International Monetary Fund (IMF) and the World Bank. In spite of all the rhetoric about a 5 per cent economic growth and the glorious projections of the IMF, the average Cameroonian is still to witness an economic miracle on his/her dining table. Because of the social and economic dislocation caused by the IMF, Cameroonians find it difficult to send their kids to school. Hospitals are bereft of drugs or, where available, the prices are prohibitively exorbitant. Despite pious proclamations about alleviating poverty, pauperisation is the order of the day. In short the standards of living are bleak; the future grim (Wache 2003: 8). Companies that had a large labour market like ALUCAM, SOSUCAM, SODECOTON, BATA, CIMENCAM are either folding or laying off their workers. The adjustment process has not only reinforced a sharp polarisation between a rich minority and a largely impoverished majority, it has raised concern about the dangers of recolonisation facing the continent (Olukoshi and Laakso 1996: 21). But was Cameroon not in a position to learn from the experiences of other countries which in the throes of economic crisis, resisted the IMF? For example China, Poland and Malaysia are three countries that ignored IMF advice and yet became successful. During the Far East crisis, Malaysia refused to take any IMF loans. Its leadership mapped a national integrated economy and within two years all was well with its economy. President Sam Nujoma of Namibia is quoted to have boasted that in 13 years as an independent country, 'we have not taken a penny from the IMF and World Bank simply because they (IMF and World Bank) are the imperialists' well-organised machinery to get African cheap labour and raw materials for their economic development' (*New African*, Nov. 2003). Instead Namibia embarks on bottom up development agendas backed by a strong impetus for regional integration. Botswana is a country that has made remarkable social and economic progress since independence in 1966. No country in the world, over a period of more than three decades has had higher growth rates like Namibia. It has 6 billion dollars on its own reserves, free education and health. Botswana's success story is based on first its Vision 2016 framework that was launched in 1996 by the first President Sir Ketumile Masire, then its sound management of its natural resources, fiscal discipline and a planning process that presents development plans with achievable goals. As for Libya its economy remains buoyant in spite of decades of international embargo because of the leader's (Muamar Gadaffi's) vision of participative economics and popular socialism. No doubt Libya *CODESRIA Bulletin,* Nos 3 & 4, 2004 Page 23 is the only country in the world with no debt. Equatorial Guinea is making positive strides in its economy since oil was discovered a couple of years ago. The fallouts of the discovery can be seen in both its human development and especially its transport network. There should be many other countries in Africa linking their endogenous macroeconomic gains with human development but whose bright economic performance does not feature on the Western media simply because they are not Bretton Woods-inspired. These countries may not be complete development models but the reality is that only countries which have their heads in the sky of globalisation and their feet firmly rooted to the grounds of localisation will achieve the long awaited Independence goals. When will Cameroon and the rest of the African countries realise that 'development is endogenous; that it can only come from within society, which defines in total sovereignty its vision and its strategy and counts first and foremost on its internal strengths?' (Lopes 1994: 37). As Adebayo Olukoshi rightly observes 'blind adherence to orthodox structural adjustment with the authoritarian political and repressive socio-economic costs which it carries, will do more harm than good to the cause of democratisation in Africa' (Olukoshi 1998: 13). Why has Cameroon surrendered its economic sovereignty to both the IMF and World Bank on the one hand, and to the phenomenon of aid and privatisation on the other hand? Schools and hospitals are built today with aid from the Japanese and the Chinese – in spite of this goodwill by foreign partners, President Museveni of Uganda remarks that aid has never developed a single African country to the stage of social transformation (*New African, Nov.* 2003). Whether in our democratic option or economic choice, Cameroon seems to implement policies it does not decide. Dependence on external aid and the Bretton Woods institutions can compromise a country's independence leading to what political scientists call 'state delegitimisation.' For like Kenneth Kaunda says 'whereas the first round of democratisation was undermined by the strength of the state, the second round is likely to be undermined by its weakness' (*West Africa,* January 1998).

African countries must depend on themselves through home-grown development models and the pursuit of the objectives of the African economic community. When this aid comes in trickles it becomes media hyped that one forgets the comparative reality between aid in Europe and that in Africa. A United Nations Development Program's (UNDP) Report 2003 shows that in the year 2000, the European Union's (EU) annual aid to sub-Saharan Africa amounted to $8 per African person while EU annual daily subsidy to EU cows was $913 per cow. The case of Japan was even more incongruous. In 2000, Japan's annual aid to sub-Saharan Africa was $1.47 per African but Japan's annual daily subsidy to its cows amounted to an astronomical $2,700 per cow (UNDP 2003: 155). So on the face of it, one would rather be a cow in Europe than a human being in Africa. As for (flawed) privatisation, it still continues to ravage Cameroon's economy. Assets like electricity, telecommunication, transport and water, gained during independence are being thrown back to colonial managers. The country's second largest employer Cameroon Development Corporation (CDC) was forced to release into privatisation one of its largest arm of production-the Cameroon Tea Estate (CTE). Only recently the CTE proved that privatisation is about profit not people. On 15 January 2004, CTE laid off 585 workers 'in a bid to reduce the company's cost of production which had soared to an unbearable level' (*The Post*, 26 January 2004). Cameroon's recognition of its economic dire straits was confirmed when it applied to join the Heavily Indebted Poor Countries (HIPC) Initiative. Experts put the unemployment rate in Cameroon at 25 per cent and more than 50 per cent of the population lives below the poverty line. Cameroon's Minister for Public Investment and Regional Planning, Martin Okouda, defined poverty in Cameroon as people not having the material or financial resources to satisfy their basic needs (food, housing, health etc.); the lack of these essential services in some localities makes not only the individual poor, but also households that would otherwise be able to afford them. Minister Okouda attributes poverty in Cameroon to bad governance, which people put down to corruption, to siphoning off public money, to impunity, to milking public services, to the lack of decentralisation and the unequal distribution of the fruits of growth (*The Courier*, July/Aug 2002). Yes, it beats all economic logic that a country that is crammed with natural wealth and skilled human resources like Cameroon should be ranked 125 out of 162 by the UNDP's 2001 Human Development Index. The 2003 UNDP report now classifies Cameroon as 'low in human development.' Of what use then is political freedom without economic emancipation? Cameroon's democracy is like its football; much ado about victories little to show in infrastructure. Democracy without development is as useless as winning football trophies, without football stadia.

Beyond Presidential 2004

What all of these comments show is that since 1990 there has been a considerable alienation between the politicians and the people–a gap temporarily closed only during elections. Apart from grotesque manifestations of condescending sympathy to the people (bags of rice, beer and bank notes) and empty slogans of commitment (build roads, schools, hospitals, power to the people) during election campaigns, will the 2004 presidential elections live on a promissory note of a permanent social contract between the politician that only thinks of the next election and people that should be thinking of the next generation? The last few months have been characterised by calls both by the ruling and opposition parties for the population to register their names in the electoral list. The government has made overtures to the Opposition parties and human rights organisation in selecting the names of future members of the National Election Observatory (as opposed to the Constitutional Council) who will be charged with supervising the presidential elections. If statistics are anything to go by, the already disillusioned electorate may not hearken to these pleas. According to reports by international observers, while about 65 per cent of the electorate took part in the 1992 presidential elections, only 25 per cent answered present in 1997 presidential elections (*The Courier*, July/August 2002). These reports see systematic boycott by the opposition, low voter registration, bias in the public media, targeted arrests and electoral fraud as traditional opium of multiparty elections in Cameroon. According to the researcher, Dr. Mamoudou Gazibo, 'the democratic process in Cameroon is terribly fragmented and riven with conflicts between the dominant party in power and an opposition divided by leadership disputes' *(The Courier*, July/Aug 2002). Furthermore, the absence of a wide-ranging debate and clearly presented opposition policies saps interest in electoral contests.

The electorate is so dismayed with present politicians on both sides of the divide that voter apathy remains high. Ntemfac Ofege attributes voter apathy to the stark realisation that Mr. Biya will always rig elections and also to the fact that the so-called opposition is full of political illiterates, unprincipled dead beats, who pretend to oppose Mr Biya when they are indeed part of the Cameroon problem (*The Post*, February 23, 2004). Accusations of lack of probity and accountability that have been heaped on the ruling regime seem to have also fallen on some of the local councillors and parliamentarians of the opposition. So what new mechanisms have been put in place to make presidential elections 2004 democracy-friendly and voter attractive? What are the ingredients in the various party manifestoes or politico-economic blueprints that guarantee the electorate that after Presidential 2004, Cameroon will expand its democratic space and redistribute its economic resources?

What are the chances that Presidential 2004 will this time, no matter the victor, reverse the pyramid of power and resources that have long been the preserve of a predatory cartel? The chances are slim and the average Cameroonian voter is tired of being a mere gesture rather than a partner in the democratic process. Since 1990, Cameroon's democratic process has been like a journey without maps. Prayer sessions and ecumenical services have been done, asking the Almighty God to intervene and save Cameroon. But God's response seems to be 'I will help those who help themselves.' It is about time Cameroonians took a break and chartered a political, social, economic and cultural map that would go beyond presidential 2004 to the year 2020. Cameroon needs not just a political transformation but also a social transformation of its society and economic upliftment of the poor. Unfortunately those who have the power to transform the society do not have the will and those who have the will do not have the power. But one cannot give up because other countries in other continents that lagged behind Africa in economic development are now tigers in world economy. Germany and Japan that were destroyed in World War II came back because of their people (Molua, 2003: 4). Cameroon may be losing its Independence assets but it has not yet mortgaged its national soul. It can still strengthen the union of brotherhood (not bondagehood cf. Bole Butake) between all Cameroonians whatever their origin. Cameroon does not need repeated elections whose results are often predictable; what Cameroon needs today is what Thandika Mkandawire and Charles Soludo propose for Africa: a system of democratic governance in which political actors have the space to freely and openly debate, negotiate and design an economic reform package that is integral to the construction of a new social contract (Mkandawire & Soludo 1999: 133). Beyond Presidential 2004 therefore is the dire need for a Pax Cameroona Congress that will focus on vision 2020.

All Cameroonian Congress

The aim of this Congress would be to provide Cameroon with a genuine democratic, development and citizenship agenda up to the year 2020. 2020 because it would have marked 30 years of Cameroon's institutionalised democratic process began in 1990. This congress could be held in 2005 marking 15 years of stock taking and giving Cameroonians another 15 years of adequate planning. These 15 years of planning, would be interrupted every five years for comparative analysis. The Congress participants would decide and define what democratic strategies and economic choices to make in order to attain both the Independence and Millennium Development goals. It would be about reconnecting the political forces and the social forces; I have also had to wonder aloud why this country should maintain the name 'Cameroon'; why should the country continue with a name imposed on it by a group of Portuguese adventurers? Simply because the Portuguese caught and ate a variety of 'crayfish' at the Wouri Estuary was no reason to have a country named after 'crayfish' prawns (cameroes) in

Portuguese or in pidgin 'njanga'. Except Cameroonians accept that they are 'njangas', the new dispensation may also demand that the country be given a new indigenous name that spells dignity, integrity and nationalism.

The congress would provide a vision born out of tolerance, moderation, intellectual honesty nonpartisan consideration and sense of realism with regard to the conduct of public affairs in Cameroon; a vision needed to provide a legal framework and foundation suitable for the construction of a new Cameroonian order. While the 1991 Tripartite conference was too election concerned, the All Cameroonian congress should have a long term and broad-minded goals. The congress must identify the challenges implied by these goals and propose strategies to meet them. Documents abound in Cameroon that have attempted to provide a durable social contract between the rulers and the governed. They may be used as references during this congress. Some of these documents include *The Political Philosophy of Ahmadou Ahidjo*, as told by Ahmadou Ahidjo, *Communal Liberalism* by Paul Biya, National Economic and Social Program (NESPROG) by the SDF, *The White Book* by Mila Assoute, *La crise économique du Cameroun* by Robert Nyom, Proposals from the Coalition for National Reconciliation and Reconstruction, and Front for Alternative Forces. This list is not exhaustive. There are also resource persons that have proposed the way forward for Cameroon either through newspaper articles or other channels. These personalities need to join other members of the political and civil society and party leaders in the All Cameroonian congress. The initiative to convene such a congress lies on the shoulders of all patriotic Cameroonians. The impetus lies on the incumbent leadership. There has indeed been little dialogue and fair play in Cameroon's multiparty democracy, even in comparison with most African countries (Nyamnjoh 2002). Cameroon must be one of the few countries in Africa where opposition leaders and members of the civil society have never publicly met with President Paul Biya. It would also be necessary to include a fresh discussion on a new constitution in the All Cameroonian congress. The 1996 constitution and other party proposals may serve as a point of entry. The outcome of this congress therefore would be a document called 'Vision 2020-framework for a long-term vision for Cameroon'.

End note: A new generation

Cameroonians born during or after independence (1960) owe a lot of gratitude to those who fought for the country's independence and who have been at the helm of state affairs since independence. Most *CODESRIA Bulletin,* Nos 3 & 4, 2004 Page 25 of those who were politically active during and immediately after independence did so when they were in the primes of their lives–almost in their thirties. Without the ultimate sacrifice of these nationalists, Cameroon's political agenda would have been completely mortgaged. Thanks to the wisdom and knowledge of those who have so far been in the corridors of power, Cameroon's image of an island of peace in an ocean of conflict is intact. It is an image that must be consolidated with deeper significance. It is therefore a natural design that the old politicians who are mostly above their fifties should start thinking of passing the mantle of leadership to the children of independence who are in their thirties and forties, today. Amadou Ahidjo born in August 1924 became Premier of Cameroon on 18 February 1958 at the age of 34. Paul Biya born on 13 February 1933 became Prime minister of Cameroon in 1975 at the age of 42 (he had already held the prestigious posts of Director of Cabinet and Secretary General at the Presidency). Ahidjo quit politics at the age of 58, Biya just celebrated his 71st birthday. The charismatic leader of the Social Democratic Front (SDF) Ni John Fru Ndi is already in his early 60s, the meticulous leader of the Cameroon Democratic Union (CDU) Adamou Ndam Njoya is in his 60s, the taciturn leader of the National Union for Democracy and Progress (NUDP) Bello Bouba Maigari has almost hit 57. One of the longest serving politicians and Secretary General of the Union des Populations du Cameroun (UPC) Pa Augustine Frederick Kodock has attained the ripe age of 80. Their names have been in the lips of the Independence children for over two decades. These politicians have for so long determined the course of this country and should now be serving as torchlights of succeeding generations. Of course, democracy is not about excluding people on the basis of age, it is even more about including people on the basis of ideas. But if one has to go by the UNDP 2001 Report that puts life expectancy for Cameroon at 50 then these politicians need to think about an early retirement to provide a smooth transition of leadership to another generation. Julius Kambarage Nyerere did it in Tanzania exposing young turks like Salim Ahmed Salim to the political limelight. Salim Ahmed Salim was Tanzania's Ambassador to the United Nations at the age of 22. Nelson Rolihlahia Mandela did it in South Africa preferring to step down in favour of younger people like Cyril Ramaphosa and Thabo Mbeki. When Sam Shafiishuna Nujoma was asked about prospects of running for a fourth term as President of Namibia he said 'You know I am growing old. Age does not wait for anybody. I am not going to run for a fourth term. I must give the chance to the young people who have the strength to run the country' (*New African*, November 2003). Examples are few because Africa's democracy still resides in the weird policy of gerontocracy. Yet politics is also about knowing when to quit especially as there are now diplomatic opportunities in the African Union and international organizations for those who have had rich diplomatic careers in their countries. The generation gap is a major political issue in Africa, an issue which hitherto has gone unnoticed, ignored or unanalysed by national and international researchers, opinion makers but the truth is that the old guard nationalists are increasingly finding themselves out of step with the younger population (Moyo 1998: 7). What is incumbent on the old leadership is to stand by the energetic youth. This past-present continuity undoubtedly will provide lessons as the new generation attempts to recuperate the disintegrating mantle of leadership (Chiabi 1997: 215). The youths must equip themselves with what I call 'Youth Power'.

According to Dibussi Tande, as the laboratory of Africa's democracy, youths should be uncompromising critics of their socio-political environment. They should be instilled with a healthy scepticism towards values that might be accepted blindly. They should adopt a way of thinking that is contrary to all forms of monolithism without being carried away by the illusions and fantasies of pluralism. They should clearly say 'no' to the utopia of the new demagogues wearing borrowed democratic robes (Tande 1992). What I propose for young people who wish to overhaul their rustic democratic machinery is to come back to the strategy of pioneer pan Africanist which is 'think African, implement national.' At the national level, youths should create broad based associations, unions, NGOs and grassroots organizations that only they can control. Addressing grassroots, national and continental problems allows youths to groom themselves towards leadership. This is the time for a new generation in Cameroon to develop leadership skills based on enduring African values (sharing not accumulating), Ubuntu philosophy (I am because we are) and respect for the old. Africa is not only losing its young and virile population to poverty, war and disease but also to Western exodus primarily because the young see the doors of opportunities closed in front of them by politicians whose future is behind them. When indeed will the Cameroonian youths of today be leaders of tomorrow? Far from being a conflict of generation, the rite of passage of the young into power is a complimentary act meant to let the young realize their own dreams. For what indeed is vision 2020 all about? It is about equipping Cameroon with a new dream that would revitalise the economy and reorient the democratic order. Vision 2020 needs new energies and fresh ideas from the Cameroonian youth. But these new energy and ideas will not come from pecuniary associations like PRESBY (President Biya's Youth) NEDY (New Deal Youths), JACHABY (Jeunesse Active pour Chantal Biya) and a host of window-dressing youth -wing party organisations. Vision 2020 shall be managed by youths who have an independent mind and those who can dare to invent the future. How the present political dinosaurs begin to involve the young political 'indomitable lions' in the pursuit of a new Cameroonian order packaged in vision 2020 will determine the success of Cameroon's democratic process begun more than a decade ago.

Note

This article first appeared as a serial in the Post newspaper, April-June 2004. The article was considered "libellous and unpatriotic" by administrative hierarchy. A month later the author was suspended from his functions as Provincial Delegate for Culture for South West Province. An administrative suspension he served for four years (2004-2008).

References

1. Ake, C., (2000), *The Feasibility of Democracy in Africa*, Dakar: CODESRIA.

2. Alou, M. T., (2002), 'Democratic Consolidation and the Future of Democratisation processes in Africa', *CODESRIA Bulletin*, Nos 3 and 4.

3. Atatah, C., 2003, 'From Rich to Heavily Indebted Poor Country', *The Post Newspaper* 7 Nov., p.11.

4. Biombi, A., 2001, 'Les présidents à vie vous saluent bien' *Mutations*, 16juillet, p.5.

5. Biya, P., 1987, *Communal Liberalism*, London: Macmillan Publishers.

6. Chiabi, E., 1997, *The Making of Modern Cameroon*, Lanham: University Press of America.

8. Davidson, B., 1991, 'What Development Model?' *Africa Forum*, vol., no. 1.

9. Mkandawire, T. and Soludo, C., 1999, *Our Continent, Our Future: African*

Meanwhile the news of my suspension went viral in the media (traditional and social) with the following comments.

Bokova congregation is under the Bova parish.

The campaign of denigration against the female pastor is said to have so angered Christians and the PCC governing board, the Synod office in Buea. Though the Synod has not yet officially commented on the quarrel, *The Herald* learnt that it has cleared the name of the female pastor. King was pastor of funds.

However, Luma and the pastor occasionally clashed over other issues in the life of the church. Many Christians are said to be disappointed at Luma's attitude towards the clergywoman. Commented one Christian: "It is true the Musonge family has contributed much toward the completion of the Bokova church [illegible]

When *The Herald* met Kinge last Monday, she said the PCC Synod office was better placed to comment on the allegation against her. Though now transferred as chaplain at PCC Buea Town she said her transfer was not connected to the allegations.

George Ngwane sacked

Cont'd from page 1

multipartism, apportioning blame on both President Paul Biya and opposition leaders. Though the articles were considered to be objective and balanced in style, the author reserved no kind words for the regime he was serving in. Many who read the articles found it hard associating some of the expressions used, with a senior serving government official.

In one article for example in which Ngwane said Biya was disliked by Cameroonians, he wrote: "Since multipartism got reintroduced in Cameroon in 1990, Cameroonians have learnt to make do with a presumptuous yet ubiquitous incumbent and an ambitious yet fragmented opposition." After quoting from Biya's Communal Liberalism to show that the president was against multipartism, Ngwane noted that Biya was only forced to accept it because of pressure from France and because the "launching of another political party (Social Democratic Front – SDF) further defied his one-party ideology." Then he went on: "Unlike other African countries like Benin (1990), Mali (1991), Zaire (1991) and South Africa (1994) that planned a transition, the leadership of Cameroon resisted any form of democratic transition." In another article Ngwane went on with his Biya-bashing, rating Ahidjo a better leader.

Ngwane: Victim of Biya's intolerance of dissent

Though Ngwane's demise comes as a surprise and disappointment to many, especially his admirers who found him a strong promoter of culture, many were rather surprised he was, in the first place, appointed to a high post by a government considered intolerant of dissent.

A high school Literature teacher who rose to vice principal of *Lycee de Kribi*, George Ngwane had never been close to the regime. He came to the limelight in 1990, after publishing a pamphlet titled *The Mungo Bridge*, an essay on the failures of reunification. He was moderator at the All-Anglophone Conference in 1993 and went on to write other books, pamphlets and newspaper articles, some of them on problems between South Westerners and North Westerners. He has equally written on pan-Africanism, especially after he created a pan-Africanist movement, Africaphonie. Mos of Ngwane's writings are proposals rather than criticisms. On the Anglophone question, Ngwane took an integrationist approach that distinguished him from the SCNC separatists.

In spite of his criticism of the Biya regime, Ngwane was a great promoter of culture, much suited to his appointment as culture delegate. He is always dressed in African attire. He proved he was a man of culture by giving almost every public ceremony in Buea a cultural touch. This year's World Book Day on 23 April was special.

In a chat with The Herald months ago, Ngwane had said: "I have a three-year development plan on culture... Culture must be alive in this province. What is required is to have the funds."

SDF criticised for abandoning Mukong

Cont'd from page 1

at the weekend to discuss the party's stand on the now quarrelsome opposition single candidate ahead of the coalition press conference today, did not take place because party officials were attending Mukong's funeral. Mukong who died on 12 July, was lowered into his grave at exactly 3pm on Saturday in front of his modern, small white isolated house in Buh village, Babanki Tungo amidst emotions from the over 3000 people who braved the muddy road. He was honoured by human rights organisations, the clergy, the SCNC and SDF as one who defended justice and democracy at a time in Cameroon when nobody could dare.

Though rain prevented most of the tributes to be presented the few presented, especially by his wife and two sons, drew emotions from almost everybody. They painted the picture of a man who fought hard for mankind fearing only God along his way. There was evidence of all the groups Mukong had belonged. In a dramatised "state" burial, the SCNC placed their white and blue flag on Mukong's coffin before later hoisting it near the grave. The SCNC that has since proclaimed an independent state and named a government often talks of "state burials" for its "statesmen." Police were not present.

Speaking at the graveside SCNC chairman, Chief Ayamba Otun regretted that, "the cold hands of death have struck a most devastating blow on the SCNC, shaking it to the roots of its foundation by snatching a cornerstone." Ayamba said that though Mukong had initially supported reunification with all his force, "he immediately started waging a one-man crusade for a return to the federal status that resulted in the creation of the SCNC."

Recalling all the active roles Mukong played in the struggle for Southern Cameroons independence, Ayamba regretted that Mukong would be unavailable to testify at the next sitting of the African court of human and people's right (ACHPR) in Banjul in the SCNC case against the government of Cameroon.

Speaking on behalf of the Human Rights Defence Group founded by Mukong in 1995, Nkwain Patrick Agiam, the acting managing director said Mukong had "a spirit deep-rooted and attached to the promotion and protection of human dignity."

Speaking earlier in a requiem mass on Friday to over 4000 people who turned out both at the mortuary and church, the vicar general of the Bamenda archdiocese, Father Ignatius Waindim described Mukong as a human rights defender who sought to give his life for others. Said he: "Mukong had the cause of human rights to fight all through his life against unjust judges." Later at the St Patrick Catholic Church, Babanki Tungo, Father Martin described Mukong as one who cared for others and was never attached to any thing.

Gideon Taka on behalf of North West Human Rights Organisations, UNOHWIHURO, said Mukong became a jailbird for many years "on political trumped-up charges" as he "fought autocratic rule and used the pen to criticise and castigate the government."

PM begs SW chiefs

Cont'd from page 1

and president Biya. Let us re-elect Mr Biya from the South West and for the South West province."

Responding to the prime minister's plea, the South West chiefs urged government to create a gas depot in Kumba which they said was the only solution to the price hikes in cooking gas and other petroleum products following the collapse of the Mungo bridge. They also called on government to cause AES SONEL to take measures towards checking the rampant power failures in the South West that have considerably affected business in that province.

The PM's envoy thanked the chiefs for their commitment toward the socio-economic and political advancement of Cameroon. Noting that SWECC contributed greatly to effect decentralization in Cameroon, Ngute said "the decentralization of our country is now an irreversible reality." He said Southwesterners, with decentralization, would feel involved in their socio-economic development.

Ngute also talked about measures the government had so far taken to ease traffic, following the collapse of the Mungo Bridge. These measures, he noted, included the arrival on 1st August of a pontoon at the collapsed Mungo Bridge that would be installed by the end of this month, to ensure a two-link crossing with a capacity of 120 tons. He said plans for the design of a new bridge with a possibility of a second crossing on a different side were underway.

Earlier, in his address, Chief S.M.L. Endeley, president of SWECC, spent time enumerating the achievements of the New Deal government in the domains of diplomacy, economy and infrastructure instead of talking about matters affecting the chiefs. Chief Esong J, SWECC Secretary General who presented a report of activities of the current chiefs leadership, hailed the government for [illegible] reality. He [illegible] the wish of the South [illegible] region with consideration given to its specificities. The chiefs ended their conference with a motion of support to, and an appeal to President Biya to announce his candidacy for the coming presidential election.

The Herald Nº 1534 Monday 2 - 3 August, 2004

Dropshot

Sam - Nuvala Fonkom

Don't blame the appointee

The Francophones are fond of the expression that administrative rank belongs to the government functionary, but posts of responsibility belong to the State. In effect, the rise of the civil servant through the ranks, barring severe disciplinary sanctions, can be taken for granted while nominations remain the discretion of hierarchy.

However, while nominations are the prerogative of the State, there ought to be certain objective criteria delineating the academic/professional qualification of the political appointee. In a case of a multiplicity of candidates for a given post, other human factors come into play such as regional balance, minority, and other civil status considerations like gender equality et cetera.

Some appointees rise through a [illegible] combination of intrigues [illegible] lobbying. Lobbying for position may not necessarily be a bad thing depending on the methods and motive [illegible]. Lobbying has become a normal practice, especially for leadership positions in international organisations where various contending nations send emissaries on whirlwind [illegible] tours to make a case for the s[illegible]ity of their candidate bearing in mind certain parameters such as qualification, experience, integrity, and geo-politics.

At local level, not many appointees engage in lobbying. In such cases, the appointee is not even consulted. Even when his opinion is sounded by agents of the political police, he is hardly aware of being earmarked for a position of authority.

Parkinson's Law of Public Administration has recorded the haphazard manner of public appointments, corporate boardroom decision-making, and observes that if advertisements were properly worded with criteria properly spelt out, there would be no reason to have more than one candidate presenting himself for recruitment for any given public office.

Consider this improvised advertisement for the job of General Manager of a public corporation in Cameroon:

a) Prospective candidates must declare their assets.
b) Candidates owning more than one house worth more than CFA 5 million francs do not qualify.
c) Candidates shall be prepared to earn no salary in the event of being chosen for the position. However, a candidate so chosen would be provided with his basic needs including the educational and medical expenses of his family.
d) Candidates must sign an undertaking not to indulge in the consumption of champagne and all other imported drinks.
e) The prospective GM shall be entitled to a short wheel based Land Rover and a Vox Wagon Beetle car.
f) Prospective candidates must present themselves for interview dressed in sports attire and tennis shoes prepared to undergo a physical exercise. Et cetera, et cetera.

According to Parkinson, it is not likely that more than one candidate would show up for the interview and in the event that two people showed up, one effective way of resolving the dilemma is to request a female secretary to cast a deciding vote.

One reason for re-examining this problem of appointments in Cameroon is the controversy sparked recently by the sacking of a cultural friend, the Mwalimu George Ngwane, as South West Provincial Delegate of Culture, who had only spent a few months in that position. I doubt if the Mwalimu and Founder/President of the Anglophone Association ever lobbied or was consulted before his appointment. Anybody who knows Mr. George Ngwane, recognises him as a free thinker who would not sell his conscience for a mess of pottage.

Some critics have opined that he is a staunch right-winger with unalloyed pro-regime sentiments. I doubt it! And even if it were the case, democracy allows for people to belong to a party of their choice. Even though I have never known the Mwalimu to militate in the ruling CPDM party, his critics say he was a deep-cover militant who was mischievously exposed by his mentors. I wonder!

I want to believe that George Ngwane, by dint of intellectual calling, had solid references to be appointed a Cultural Delegate, and that a certain interest group might have lobbied for his appointment irrespective of his personal ambitions. Perhaps his interest group believed that by appointing him, he would automatically be converted into the regime's praise-singing class. Unfortunately, his promoters failed to grasp the man's liberal constitution and he, the appointee, failed to comprehend what the hierarchy expected of him, a hierarchy that assumes that every appointee, even those [illegible] nominated by merit, must automatically become members of the cabalistic clan of subalterns and [illegible].

The haphazardness that characterises certain appointments in Cameroon can be illustrated by the following examples. After the 2002 twin election, a certain Aoudou was appointed Minister of Mines a couple of days after he was sacked as Financial Controller in the North for alleged misappropriation of State funds.

The [illegible] of appointments are not usually negative, yet haphazard. Around the mid 1990s, a certain Kima was appointed Minister of Mines and Power. I happened to be anchoring the news on the national station of Radio Cameroon the day the cabinet list was brought to us in the newsroom. The name of the Minister was simply stated as Kima, and it was handwritten in black ink. The story even goes that a number of Kimas including my dear friend, Prince Kima, showed up in Yaounde's corridors of power to be endorsed, not knowing that the nominated was non other than Chief Michael Kima.

Mwalimu George Ngwane

Only recently, appointments were made to [illegible] under the tutelage of the Ministry of Territorial Administration. A highly qualified gentleman was appointed Director of the Local Government Training Centre — so-called CEFAM — and the decree read Madame so and so. The stroke of the royal pen can transform a Madame to a Monsieur. No quarrel with a "mistake" of a pen, but suffice to observe that even the President of the Republic can be induced or misled to endorse with his pen documents he cannot be humanly expected to scrutinise.

While we appreciate the intrigues, complications and aggravations [illegible] appointments in Cameroon can attract [illegible] we can borrow a leaf from the Southern Cameroons Civil Service Commission (which was obviously not perfect) where appointments to positions of authority were advertised and [illegible] all in a bid to enhance the notion of meritocracy.

The point of this Dropshot is that there are very competent servants of the people to be found in any political grouping in every society, and no amount of political coloration can adulterate the integrity of the upright. So be it!!!

Antoine Bell and electoral jingles

The jingle bells of Antoine Bell [illegible] the endorsement of incumbent President Paul Biya [illegible] view of the October presidential [illegible] election is obviously in rotten taste.

We heard Mr. Bell over the BBC the other day justifying his choice and that of a so-called "Anciennes Gloires." If I had to trumpet Mr. Paul Biya's bid for re-election, I would be decent enough to be honest, not tricky.

Mr. [illegible] a very talented footballer [illegible] of whether he scored goals or caught an inflated leather [illegible] told a BBC reporter (in English!) that his choice and that of a hundred other veteran footballers for incumbent Paul Biya's re-election after 22 years in power is informed by the consideration that President Paul Biya is a "rotten fruit."

Mr. Antoine Bell, who spoke on behalf of an ad hoc group of veteran football players averred that since Cameroon's political market was full of rotten fruits, it did not matter which fruit was picked up (not picked). In effect, and I quote, "When you go to a market where the majority of fruits are rotten, the likelihood is that what you are going to pick up is a rotten fruit."

Asked if he did not think there was an alternative to pick for the leadership of Cameroon, Mr. Antoine Bell averred again that there was no alternative except a rotten fruit.

Dropshot has no problem with Antoine Bell's choice of rotten fruit. If all political fruits in Cameroon are rotten, then Mr. Antoine Bell is right. But he is wrong because not all the fruits of Cameroon women are rotten. Unless the Cameroon women have a contrary view.

If we have to analyse Mr. Bell's role as spokesperson for an ad hoc group called "Anciennes Gloires," then I would want to ask one or two questions. We know that Antoine was an inmate in the Buea Prisons. We know that Antoine demonstrated a football talent in Buea Prisons where the philosophy of human rights, social rehabilitation, were the principle of detention and incarceration. It can also be established that Antoine was incarcerated for criminal offences, yet he was rehabilitated by then Prisons Director, Pa Richard Titang.

So now we have an Antoine Bell, who was spotted by Pa Titang during a normal recreational sporting activity in the Buea Prisons, and who recommended him for parole and later co-opted him in the renowned Prisons Football Club of Buea. Bell later became a football star and hero. For the very Antoine to forget the socio-psychological and cultural conditions of his rehabilitation to be making unconscionable statements concerning political leadership in Cameroon on behalf of a hitherto group called "Anciennes Gloires" who unfortunately did not bring any glory to this country, can only be seen as the promotion of complacency.

For one thing, we may not blame Antoine Bell. We are made to understand that this ex-inmate of Prisons Buea is a Rosicrucian Frater of Paul Biya. Rosi Crusae (forgive my spelling) is purported to be a fraternity of intellectuals, philosophers, et cetera. I am extremely disappointed to have observed that Mr. Antoine Bell spoke to the BBC as a sycophant, not as a fellow steeped in matters profound.

If Antoine Bell can still catch a ball and re-establish his enviable position as a goal keeper, then he should keep all the criminals in Cameroon as jail keeper.

The House on the anthill
(for Mwalimu George Ngwane)

The Party makes aluminium crowns
And puts them on the
Heads of
Toad-eaters, in tyrannised, robotic space

Their minds now work like a
Cart wheel, going
Round and round
In circles.
Our body decays while we are alive.

When armed robbers in the guise of
Provincial Governors cover their eyes with dark glasses
And shout big, meretricious
Slogans;

WE ARE A DEMOCRATIC
AND UNITED COUNTRY

Don't worry
Gluttony has been the death of those
Who make good appear evil,
Who find fault with the
Noblest actions

And plough
The ground to sow seeds of
Injustice

Don't be jealous of a
Festering, carrion's success, you
Do not know what disaster awaits him

Idols are
Dressed in purple robes

Like Emperor Bedel Bokassa, but
They
Cannot keep themselves
From

Being tarnished
Or protect themselves
From
Termites.
See how useless they are!
They can't walk on their own feet, but
must be carried around.

Even if you suffer humiliation, Be
Patient
Great things often have small
And humble beginnings; but they

Survive, grow steadily, and
Flower

By Bate Besong
Source: www.batebesong.com (11th August 2006)

Buea,
26 July 2004

Hi brother,

I felt it was necessary to call and have a chat with you before leaving, considering what has befallen you "as a result of writing in a small country" like ours.

All I want to say is "take heart and brave" whatever decision the "big man" wants to take. If "we" cannot prevent it from happening, "we" should instead bravely give way for it to take its course. But...

Perhaps we should let them "handle the wheel" the way they please. Whether it means they turn the wheel towards a boiling ocean for all of us to perish... "silence" might be the "best action" in "our small country". After all, do many in this country not cling to the primitive phylosophy of "Na me one I go change Cameroon"?

Please, let us allow them to RULE THE WAY THEY LIKE,... for the sake of our children. For the sake of our children,... and concentrate on call it big areas of intellectual development. It is clear that our country is not yet ripe for a certain type of intellectual exercises — that which "pricks". You can see the hidden meaning of rigour and moralisation from acts such as this.

Please, do let me know the outcome; send me an email.

Beware those who smile with you too often, and seek to know what you are doing in the area of writing; Most who read you ONLY PRETEND to do so because they enjoy reading what you write about. LET THEM WRITE!!!... and create the type of "model" and "taste" that they think is good for "Our small country".

We should not let ourselves get too sapped by the "heat" that results from our effort to "correct", for "correcting" is seen as "hurting" by the feeble-minded, exploitative...

My mind is unsettled... Just pick out the words and get my message!

With love
Ekpe

Here are the social media reactions to my suspension:

Joel E. Kalle said...
Hello Baalzac,

Long time. I am eternally sorry at the turn of events this way and my failure to pay attention to things that matter. Your name came up in a meeting I attended recently. Donno if you will see this message but please write back if you are able. My love to all in the family.

"Kami"

Reply September 21, 2006 at 01: 59 PM

Hansel Masango said...

I'm not surprised by what has happened. Mr. Ngwane speaks on a very important issue, which should call for change of ways, beginning from individuals. I think of him as the Friend of Justice, and all those who bear this title are enemies to Friends of injustice.

Reply June 17, 2005 at 01: 16 PM

Nkongho Charles said...

I don't know Mr Ngwane, but I am confident, as most of you already comment that he is a scholar and academician. I am sure he must be a man of distinction, well read and an excellent writer.

However, I really think you have all missed the point and the reason why he was suspended from his functions or sacked from his post. There is one cardinal rule of politics. That is if you want to criticise the government or your political party, then you should not be in that government. Mr Ngwane's ideas may be great and progressive but once he has been appointed to a political post, he cannot use that platform to bite the finger that feeds him.

Correct me if I wrong, but I know the position of a provincial delegate is a political appointment. No one should use that position to launch scathing attacks at the leader of the political party. This will act as an unnecessary distraction.

We should all remember that he was appointed to work with and not against the political party and the government.

If Mr Ngwane was employed as a lecturer or a computer technician in a ministry, I don't think he would have lost his job. This is because he will be considered as an ordinary civil servant.

I am sorry to say you cannot have it both ways. Mr Ngwane was not just a member of the club, but he was one of the top managers within the system. He must therefore leave the system to be effective in his campaign. In the UK and USA, just to mention a few, all top politicians must toe the party line. If they feel so strongly about an issue, they usually vent their anger and resign. That is what Mr Ngwane should have done.

I don't think anyone is trying to censor what Mr Ngwane wrote. Correct me if I am wrong. He was not put in prison. The newspaper was not banned. Thank goodness for Cameroon democracy. I am not saying the system is perfect. No system is perfect. Mr Ngwane can go and form his own political party if he wants to really criticise the government or his political leader. He is free to do so and shout his good ideas from the mountain top. No one will stop him.

The government has not destroyed Mr Ngwane as most of you claim. The government is simply saying to him to go and exercise his democratic right somewhere else but not within the exclusive club of the top managers of the country. Mr Ngwane, should get back to his real task of being a scholar and an academician and writing more books. I believe his ideas, if not accepted by the present political system, will be adapted by different political systems in the country for all our good in the future.

I don't know the full facts of the case, but I believe the best way to effect change within the system is to do so silently within the system. If you are employed by a system, you must demonstrate unity to the outside world and the country. That does not mean you agree with everything. We all have different ideas about what is right. However, to wash your dirty linen in public and tell everyone how terrible your colleagues are, does not command a lot of respect from those who employ you, it will not win you friends, and most important of all, it will deprive you of the goodwill listening ears you need to make change happen. Politics is a tough game and you must learn the rules before you begin to play. If it was the bad old days or somewhere in the Middle East, Mr Ngwane will now be lamenting in a terrible prison somewhere without any sunlight. We have progressed from those days.

I am grateful for the progress we are making as a nation and shame to all those who only see Cameroon as the "poorest, most corrupt, least developed, disease infested country on earth". You should be ashamed of yourself. Why don't you try to do something about it?

At least Mr Ngwane is writing books, giving us ideas, and making us think about the future. I will thank him for his thought provoking books that precipitate debate. The fact that these books are free for everyone to read is the real democracy. Democracy is not defined by leaving people in cushy jobs, no matter what they say against their political colleagues and employers.

In my opinion, the actual article by Mr Ngwane that resulted to all the kerfuffles was not at all inspiring. It's a very simple view, and there may be an element or a lot of truth in the article. However, the intellectual value or accuracy of the article is not what is in question. The real question whether he is fit to work within a government if he criticises that government in public? The answer is NO. Any government will sack him if he is acting as a distraction to government policy. That does not necessarily imply that the government policies are right. Contrary to the popular believe, and the majority view in this message board, my view is that the suspension or sacking of Mr Ngwane has nothing to do with democracy or any "macabre regime" as someone puts it. It is the reality of politics anywhere around the world, and that includes Europe, UK, and the Americas.

I look forward to reading Mr Ngwane's books with interest.

I hasten to add that I do not belong to any political group or interest and this is just a personal view.

Reply December 18, 2004 at 05: 13 AM

Bate AGBOR-BAIYEE said...

Comrade, my Brother, Mwalimu- keep up the fire! You are that voice for a lot of us the voiceless. Your voice is power to a lot of us the powerless- Your power is the light to a lot of us the down trodden proletariats. At a time when even some of our 'trusted' and so-called intellectual and political men of steel swing from one political spectrum to the other grand standing, patronizing and self-seeking, you have proven to be the 'last man standing'. You have refused to be bought by a rotten and smelling system, and, for that you will indelibly go down into the annals. You are a firebrand truth-teller of the retrogressive night-side democracy in Cameroon/Africa. The current infelicitous move to suspend you by the macabre regime is yet another proof of our dead-end politics. Through you Mwalimu Ngwane, we will prevail. The tides of time wash away even the deepest despair and obstacle. This regime may hand you a bitter pill, but as it has turned oputin the past, it is the very medicine that gives you vision, strength and direction. I am hopeful, Claude Ake, a revered African political- economist once said that we have to be hopeful in life-for life without hope is meaningless.

Clearly Mwalimu, you are the unrelenting hope in our horizon.

Amandla!

Baté AGGBOR-BAIYEE

Reply November 20, 2004 at 06: 51 PM

Innocent Awasom said...

I am not surprised that this is happening to Bro. George. When I got the information that he was appointed Provincial

Delegate of culture, I was more than surprised. What must be happening to our dear country Cameroon that somebody who is very outspoken in his constructive criticism of the policies of the ruling junta be appointed to such a position of responsibility? In Cameroon with a few exception, government appoints stooges and praise singers so mediocrity triumphs. Le Cameroon c`est le Cameroon, I sighed and started dreaming of how we were going to work together to revamp our decaying Public Library system. Actually a grant proposal is almost at its completion as I do this posting but we will not relent. The work still goes on and sometimes I see giant strides being made in times of adversity.

Being the Mwalimu aka teacher that he is, I`m sure he would have revamped and resuscitated the Ministry of Culture but be that as it may ... He still got his head and brains intact so watch out for him.

When will Cameroon stop wasting talent, because of divergent political views? When will this attack on academic and intellectual freedom end?

Keep up the fight brother, and I`m taking the news to other quarters. We should all sharpen our pens, minds and brains get the truth out. The PEN is mightier than the SWORD any day any time.

Aluta continua, victoria ascerta

Reply August 31, 2004 at 11: 22 AM

Jonah Nebengu said...

It is really disturbing to hear or see how academicians are being destroyed by the government that is claiming to be democratic. What time of democracy are we actually practising here in Cameroon when we can't say, do or write what we want to? Well maybe his appointment as provincial delegate was a calculated attempt to buy him over. Because the government knows who George Ngwane and his philosophy is all about.

QUESTIONS: What's the step forward after this threat? How can i get this book "Fragment of Unity? I like it.

Reply August 13, 2004 at 09: 29 AM

Bryce Epie said...

Sometimes the TRUTH hurts, but in the long run lies hurt even more. Mr. Ngwane, your article is a call to conscience in Cameroon, whether we accept this or not. You've been a dedicated freedom fighter; you've always made human dignity a central part of your life and surely that is what makes you the better teacher you are, and what also gives you that rare sense of nobility.

The Anglophone child in Cameroon has no room to make compromise, because his store of advantages is too limited. He must press without any retreat, for greater equality. We know that for a true democracy combating evil and advancing the GOOD are a must. No doubt, these demand a lot of strength, but then, Gandhi (1920) succinctly reminds us that 'strength doesn't come from physical capacity. It comes from an indomitable will'. You are perfectly right in what you are doing, and you need not bother about what the 'Joe public' thinks of it, as i quote Gandhi again 'in matters of conscience the law of the majority has no place'. Cameroon is sick, the land of our Forefathers is troubled, but i know, somehow, that you are almost on the threshold of a new dawn. A dawn that will undoubtedly make the present squalor and marginalization moribund.

In my opinion, your writings are a means to re-awaken a sense of 'moral shame' in the leadership of our country, and the end of it will be heavenly redemption. Mwalimu, your suspension is an indication that you are getting closer to the reward at the end of the rope. And all those who use secular power to perpetuate injustice will be made to face justice, someday sooner than they may expect, unless the SON of MAN didn't resurrect.

We all know that 'truth will always triumph'!

Reply August 06, 2004 at 08: 27 AM

Charles Taku said...

I agree entirely with the previous writer. Rather than the suspension having the effect those who conceived and implemented it intended, it is rather making many who hitherto did not know Mwalimu George Ngwane to know him. It has also made those who already know him to strive to know him better. And it has made those who know him better to have a further look at his vision and record; his literary works and the philosophy behind it and say here comes at last some good emerging in our midst. I believe that his persecutors will also have the benefit of knowing the man better.

George is a soul mate of mind, a fellow crusader for the relevance of the black race in a new humanity. Indeed, George is one who relentlessly places his God given genius at the service of mankind. Such a person with profound, yet humble convictions cannot be a victim of the entrapment of office. George's attempt to maintain a free mind and spirit in the reclamation of the public service for the true owners, who are the people, has earned him what looks like a sanction from the predators who are holding us hostage. But this has vindicated George's crusade for freedom in all aspects including the universally acclaimed freedom of thought enshrined in all Human Rights Conventions as well as its charter to which Cameroon has subscribed. This act of hostility towards the exercise of fundamental human rights portrays Cameroon as a country as a pariah country that refuses to respect its treaty obligations by wanting to legislate or decree the thought process of its citizens. George has once more led by example by saying no to this blackmail and bigotry.

Taku

Reply July 30, 2004 at 12: 38 PM

Uche Eze Nkatta Idika said...

"And an order was passed, that let there be a suspension , and a suspension was slam on the genuine scholar, Mwalimu George Ngwane" Such a stupendous calamity like the suspension of Mwalimu George only emphasises that, the only thing man has learn from history is that man has never learnt from history.

History holds it a truism, that whenever a genuine intellectual is persecuted, the incumbent is discredited and loses fame. It tells the world that the tenets of Democracy are not in play is such a polity. When will Cameroon drop the attributes of patrimonialism and spoil system for real democratic principles?

It's but obvious that Mwalimu George Ngwane is under emotional stress now, but I am convinced, it will last only for a moment. He had endured difficult times in the past especially after he published "The Mungo Bridge". I have one thing to say to anybody who is helping to destroy the intellectual class: " Let the heavens fall, let the earth, quakes, let man wail, let the animals tamper to the four corners of the world, but let it be known, that men of principles will always stand by their principles.

Life is not all about positions, promotions and money. Morality and uprightness also counts. God has made two things as judges of human actions, conscience and history. History will never let us go free, if we destroy our intellectuals. We shall have to answer for it someday. Just like what happened in Nigeria two weeks ago where, THIRTY-SEVEN years after sending Nobel laureate Professor Wole Soyinka to prison, former Head of State, Gen. Yakubu Gowon of Nigeria, tendered a public apology. We hope this doesn't happen to Cameroon. We should all remember that, the way we'll make the bed of our country today, so shall our own children lie on it tomorrow.

"Be Your Own Advocate, If Not For You Now, For Those You put Into The World Of Initial Disadvantage, And Let The Everyday Miracle Of God's Benevolence Be Fulfilled In The Scriptures That Said -Seek And You Will Find, Ask And It Will Be Given"....Albert Womah Mukong (RIP)

Reply July 29, 2004 at 05: 07 PM

Charles Taku said...

I am not surprised by this treacherous act of censorship and intimidation. Indeed, it was expected by a regime that had come to the end of the road. The appointment of George Ngwane almost gave credibility to this regime. There was reasonable debate in reasonable international circles that at last the government was becoming sensitive to the appeal of the alternative Cameroon to which the majority of the suffering masses belong, to appoint one of theirs to a position of responsibility based on competence and intellectual appeal. I found criticisms of this regime contradicted by the fact that a very prolific writer and competent social thinker had been appointed to the position of delegate of culture. As one who knows George for long, I found it difficult for once to answer those who held these views.

Since a tiger does not change its spot, I was confident that George would be sent packing once the regime realised that they could not circumscribe him. And I told them so. At last I was right and I will inform the world so. George did not become a writer of international appeal by administrative fiat or decree. George did not found AFRICAphonie by administrative fiat or presidential decree. Yet it is the attempt to circumscribe and control such personal achievements that God Almighty has blessed our brother with that is the object of the present perfidy.

When George, Bate Besong, my humble self and a few others conceived and called the All Anglophone Conference in April 1993, the intention was to give back to a people the pride and vision that once informed a conscious but betrayed choice. Since then, we have been admired and vilified by friends and foes alike. Yet we shall never relent. We shall never relent or bow to intimidation and blackmail because we care for Africa and people of our race. We care for the alternative Cameroon; Cameroon of the poor, the depraved and wretched of the earth to which George and I belong. Reason why the current battle of choice declared against writers, men of arts and culture; indeed free thinkers the world over, under the pretext of vexatious, childish and perfidious accusations against George is at the centre of our very survival. Reason why, indeed it is a battle between those who crave for a Cameroon that must be bled dry in the next seven years and those of us who crave for a Cameroon of the future. As we welcome the challenge posed by our adversaries by putting the head of George Ngwane on the line, let us not forget that this battle has little to do with George Ngwane as an individual. It is indeed a battle for the soul of Cameroon, our Cameroon Vs their Cameroon. If in appointing George they thought they had duplicated the successful coup they carried out against Ferdinand Oyono by turning art on its head then they have failed and miserably too. If their intention was to buy George's conscience and turn him into a campaign stooge for whosoever and for whatever agenda, then they need to start doubting their oracles. George, your books and ideas are a blessing to the world. They are the pride of the black race.

The traitors might have had the first but surely not the last laugh. Be sure your creative talents will be reward at the appropriate time and place soon. And your persecutors like those currently persecuting our friend Bate Besong will find themselves without a false God who can replace apportion talent by decree. And this will come to pass very soon because the God we worship is a God of Justice. The way you have conducted yourself in office in so short a time will compel a serious look when Cameroon shall surely return to its true owners either now or in seven years.

Charles Taku

Lead Defence Counsel

United Nations International Criminal Tribunal for Rwanda.

Reply July 26, 2004 at 11: 53 AM

Felix Agbor Nkongho said...

The Biya junta is really not willing to change its monolithic tactics and its repression on freedom of expression in spite of its cosmetic liberal laws of 1990. The suspension of Mr. George Ngwane is a glaring example of the fact that the ruling Junta is not prepared to relinquish power and also that dissenting views shall not be tolerated. It is my opinion that Ngwane was very objective in the article and he showed a high sense of intellectual honesty. As someone I personally know, I can vouch to the fact that he will not be deter by such suspension. As a genuine intellectual in the Fonlonian sense of the term, Ngwane has always used his knowledge for the benefit of our society. We all stand by you in this difficult period. The attitude of the government in its treatment of Ngwane really discourages some of us in the Diaspora willing to one day return home to contribute towards nation building.

Reply July 23, 2004 at 01: 07 PM

Valentine Ngwa said...

How typical of a government that expects its citizens to say and write only what it wants to hear; and what it wants to hear is what has made us to be one the poorest, most corrupt, least developed, disease infested country on earth. George Ngwane's article calls for a deep reflection and commitment to change by all Cameroonians, especially the youths, if we intend to stop living in the national lie that is mostly responsible for our present situation. One just has to wonder how long our very irresponsible people in authority think they can stifle the truth.

Reply July 23, 2004 at 12: 54 AM

Well and in the mean time I found a small office in the National Archives Buea reading old West Cameroon newspapers and chatting with the Archivist late Mr Mbain Henry. I went to Yaounde on a number of occasions to find out when the suspension has to be lifted but the Secretary General of the Ministry would ask me. "Have we suspended your salary as well? I would say No! He would then ask "Then what is your problem?" I was now waiting for the day I shall be called to the

Discipline Council and at the same time sharpened my pen into other writing ventures. I wrote this Memorandum to the South West Chiefs

MEMORANDUM TO SOUTH WEST CHIEFS ON THE OCCASION OF "SWECC" EXTRA ORDINARY GENERAL ASSEMBLY 30TH – 31ST JULY 2004 FROM THE DELEGATION OF CULTURE SOUTH WEST PROVINCE

Your Royal Highnesses,

It is with great honour that the Delegation of Culture sends this memorandum to you.

As custodians of culture, traditional chiefs have a special role in the development of culture in our Province and a special collaborative bond with the Delegation of Culture.

We wish through this memo to refresh your minds on the special duties conferred on you by virtue of your role as cultural locomotives.

I. Divisional Cultural Festival.

We suggest that whenever you are holding your general Assembly, a cultural festival by the host Division and featuring some of the rare traditional dance groups be exhibited on the eve of your conference.

II. Tradimodern Architectural Palaces.

We suggest that your palaces represent the artistic and aesthetic values of our Province. This can be done through the use of local material and design for building. Palaces in the West, North West and Northern Provinces demonstrate this deep attachment to their cultural heritage.

III. Palace Museums.

Our cultural patrimony will die except you preserve it in the form of museums. We suggest that your palaces include museums that will store art objects, traditional attire and other valuable artefacts.

IV. Reviving Indigenous Knowledge

We suggest that during the third term holidays you promote the organisation of Holiday classes for students on home languages, history of the tribe, birth, death, marriage, initiation rites etc.

Your Royal Highnesses, Thanks for your attention

On behalf of the Delegation of Culture.

On September 6th 2004, I published a new book "Way Forward for Africa" and had it launched at the British Council Yaounde. I was placed on two different occasions on the honours column called "Les Gens" due to the creative work I continued doing even after my suspension.

older persons play in their families, communities and societies.

Judo - A one-day national forum on Judo took place last Saturday in the campus of the National Institute of Youth and Sports. It was organised by the Cameroon Judo federation (FECAJUDO) and brought together over 100 participants form all parts of the country.

MONDE

RDC - Le Conseil de sécurité des Nations unies a approuvé vendredi à l'unanimité de ses membres une résolution prévoyant un renfort de 5.900 hommes pour la force de maintien de la paix en République démocratique du Congo. Le texte élargit en

deportation of 600 American teenagers. Officials inspected the centres in the northern towns of Ensenada and Rosarito and found that many of the youths had come into Mexico as tourists.

Guinée Bissau - le président de Guinée Bissau, Henrique Rosa, a appelé les Nations Unies à retirer leur mission de consolidation de la paix en estimant que la situation de son pays ne la justifie plus. Selon les déclarations de M. Rosa dans un hebdomadaire de Bissau, Gazeta de Noticias, la présence des forces de l'ONU depuis cinq ans donne aux observateurs internationaux l'impression que la situation politique en Guinée Bissau reste instable.

féminin par le Nigeria,

pétition, avec deux victoires, meilleures performances. deux nuls et une défaite. Nos

Talk Shop — Presidential or Ministerial?

In many democracies, all candidates for the presidency have one objective : to win. In Cameroon, however, the situation seems to be different. More than a dozen candidates eyeing the post of President do not seem to have this ambition. Proof of this is the fact that they now focus their attention on what compensation they will have after the election.

From their utterances, they seem to be telling the winner: "please do not forget to include me in your government once you settle at Etoudi". One candidate was even more direct. He clearly stated the Ministry which he would like to handle. He might be right anyway. He may just be "cutting his coat according to his size".

TCHE Irene MORIKANG

Les gens

After demise

Henri Ntoupendi

Au cours de la cinquième session du Conseil d'administration de l'Union africaine des télécommunications (UAT) qui vient de se tenir à Naïrobi au Kenya, les administrateurs ont élu à l'unanimité M. Henri Ntoupendi, chef de la délégation camerounaise à ces assises, à la présidence du conseil d'administration de l'UAT pour l'exercice 2004-2005.

Henri Ntoupendi est chef de la cellule de suivi au ministère des Postes et Télécommunications, président de la commission de passation des marchés d'investissement à Camtel, et membre du conseil d'administration de la SOPECAM. Depuis 1998, il participe assidûment aux sessions du conseil d'administration de l'UAT. Il en a profité pour tisser un réseau de relations étroites avec les principaux acteurs des télécommunications en Afrique. Ses qualités de diplomate lui ont ainsi permis de conquérir l'estime des représentants de la majorité des Etats membres de l'UAT. Réduire le fossé numérique qui sépare l'Afrique des pays riches est le défi qu'il entend au cours de son mandat.

George Ngwane

On seven good occasions, George Ngwane, through his writings, has stimulated the intellect and raised issues that can systematically spur development in its diverse spheres in Cameroon, Africa and the world. This illustrious son of Cameroonian extraction, has once more demonstrated his intellectual prowess and Pan-African spirit in his latest publication, "Way Forward for Africa". If the groundswell of African Nationalism manifested today across the continent, is anything to go by, George Ngane's book will certainly serve as a powerful lobby for an All African People's Congress, a market place for ideas that can pressurise governments into charting a prosperous agenda for the continent.

Coup d'Griff'

Chassez l'intrus

Il y a bien quelques années que le grand-père a perdu sa place dans la famille camerounaise. Et ça ne s'arrange pas. Tant qu'il a encore sa pension retraite et sa vieille Mercedes, pas de problème. Mais dès qu'il ne peut plus s'assumer, tout est fait pour le tenir à une distance raisonnable. Les couples, pour éviter de se déchirer sur la question, ont trouvé des parades. La journée internationale des personnes âgées, célébrée vendredi, a permis de constater par exemple, que les maisons d'accueil des vieillards commencent à s'intégrer dans le paysage social du Cameroun.

Alors, si vous prenez votre retraite aujourd'hui, gagnez du temps en fonçant droit au village, construire même à la hâte, une case en terre battue. Parce que, si ce n'est pas votre fils qui voit mal la perspective de vous installer chez lui, ce sera sa femme. Ou même ses enfants adorés. Dans l'un ou l'autre des cas, vous ne tarderez pas à réaliser que vous n'êtes plus la priorité. Et c'est bien triste.

Yves ATANGA

cancer patients. The walk will take-off at the May 20 Boulevard at 7:00 a.m.

Socaped : La société camerounaise de Pédiatrie organise son XI e congrès du 25 au 27 novembre prochain. Les assises qui se tiendront à Limbé permettront aux professionnels de l'enfance de discuter des questions relatives à la qualité de vie de l'enfant handicapé ou atteint de maladie chronique en vu de les protéger et assurer leur survie.

HYPERLINK - Deux leaders de l'opposition ont été condamnés mardi par la justice du Malawi à 20 mois de prison pour sédition et incitation à la violence avant les élections générales qui se sont déroulées en mai.

Colombie - Neuf militaires ont été tués dans la nuit de lundi à mardi en Colombie lors d'affrontements avec la guérilla des Farc dans le Sud-Ouest du pays, a-t-on appris auprès d'un porte-parole de l'armée.

Rejoicing While Conveying Corpse

A friend made this comment: "The way people are dying nowadays like Christmas fowls is a serious cause for concern." Right or wrong, we are yet to carry out a survey but how many do shed tears these days when someone dies? Your boss may not even give you an overdraft if it's meant for burial. Your intimate friends may not even ask the cause of your relative's death. All pieced together, we were not enthused when some individuals instead exhibited joy while transporting a corpse from Limbe to the village on a Friday. The deceased may have been a witch, or a boss who was a "terror" to his staff. As they rejoiced, no one can tell if, on the Judgment Day, the deceased will like Lazarus instead sit on the right hand side of the Lord or not.

Peter EFANDE

Les gens

Martin Mouaha

En voici un qui a pensé à la catégorie des oubliés de la société qu'on nomme les prisonniers. A la faveur de la célébration le 14 novembre prochain, de la journée internationale du diabète, Martin Mouaha a lancé hier, à travers l'Association des diabétiques du Cameroun (ADIACAM) dont il est le président, une séance de dépistage du diabète, de l'hypertension artérielle et de l'obésité, au sein de la population carcérale de Kondengui. Pendant quatre jours, son groupe et lui seront aux côtés des plus de mille détenus concernés par la campagne qui intervient après un drame dont a été victime un détenu diabétique à qui l'association rendait visite en prison. Cette action vise à révéler aux prisonniers leur statut pour « qu'ils le sachent au moins », indique le bienfaiteur, lui-même diabétique depuis plus de 25 ans. Il a la bénédiction et le soutien du ministère de la Justice. Il entend pérenniser son combat.

Nwalemu George Ngwane

There is an adage which says if you want to hide something from an African, write it down in a book. Yet there are many who think that they cannot be quitters and would go to any length to break the cycle of laziness that runs through the society as far as reading is concern. Nwalemu George Ngwane, a prolific writer and Pan-Africanist based in Buea, the South West Region knows the treasure found in books and takes the pain regular to carry his message to the primary and secondary schools through a book donation. Recently, the man of culture offered 2.100 books to head teachers thanks to a fruitful collaboration he has with the International Book Project (IBP) based in the United States of America. Nwalemu has done this before and what attracts much attention is the constant nature of his gesture and all he needs to know is that what matters is not being at the top but being able to fight and maintain the top position.

Coup d'Griff'

Téléboutique du ministère

Vous avez remarqué que dans certains ministères, il y a parfois de la lumière jusqu'à 22h ? Et vous avez sans doute plaint ces fonctionnaires consciencieux, maintenus au bureau si tard, loin de leurs femmes et enfants. C'est certainement vrai pour une partie d'entre eux.

Mais c'est connu, beaucoup d'autres attendent justement le soir pour transformer le téléphone de service en cabine publique. Charité bien ordonnée, ils commencent par se servir. Un appel aux Etats-Unis, trois en France, deux en Angleterre. Et pour terminer, une bonne dizaine au pays, sur portables ou fixes, peu importe. Ensuite, on peut passer le combiné à trois ou quatre ami(e)s venu(e)s pour ça. Et qui feront le même tour de leurs tontons et tantines éloignés. Résultat : une facture mensuelle de téléphone de 1,5 milliard. Devinez qui va payer !

Après le recensement, il faudra peut-être penser à fermer tous les bureaux avant 19h. Surtout qu'après ces coups de fil, il s'y passe d'autres choses encore plus compliquées…

Yves ATANGA

2 CAMEROON TRIBUNE

On October 22 2004, I received this letter from the Institute of International Education's Scholar Rescue Fund granting me Fellowship as a Scholar at risk to carry out my intellectual work in any host University outside my country.

INSTITUTE OF INTERNATIONAL EDUCATION Scholar Rescue FUND

Via email to gngwane@yahoo.com

Mr. George Ngwane
P.O. Box 364
Buea, South West Province
Republic of Cameroon

October 22, 2004

Dear Mr. Ngwane:

Congratulations! I am very pleased to inform you that your application to the Institute of International Education's Scholar Rescue Fund ("Fund") has been successful.

As you know, the Fund provides temporary, matching-sum fellowships to help support scholars from *any country*, in *any discipline*. The fellowships are intended to permit scholars to continue their work at host universities, colleges, or other research institutions *outside of the scholar's home country* for a period of *up to one year*.

At its most recent meeting the Fund's selection committee approved your application for a fellowship. The award is subject to the following terms:

1. The fellowship is for a period of up to one year and in most cases is not renewable. In exceptional circumstances, the Fund will consider on a case-by-case basis requests for renewal for up to one additional period.

2. As a fellowship candidate, you are expected to identify and seek an invitation from a suitable host institution outside of your home country. Host institutions within the same region as the scholar's home country are preferred, although the fellowship may be used to support a visit to a suitable institution anywhere outside of the home country. If you do not yet have an invitation from a host university, we would suggest you contact colleagues in your field at suitable universities to see if they would be able to arrange an invitation for you to their institution. You may share with them a copy of this letter explaining the purpose and terms of the fellowship. If you are unable to arrange an invitation on your own, Scholar Rescue Fund staff will work with you to try to identify a suitable host, including working in partnership with the Scholars at Risk Network to arrange a position at one of the Network's member institutions. Our resources, however, are limited, so I urge you to pursue all potential opportunities you are able to identify.

3. The host institution is expected to match or exceed the contribution of the Fund to the support of the visit, generally through direct financial contribution of equal or greater value in the form of salary or stipend. Some in-kind contributions such as housing, meals, research assistance, tuition or training subsidies, office, computer and communications support may also qualify as matching contributions. Institutions lacking financial resources to offer the expected matching contribution, especially those in less developed countries, may seek a waiver of this requirement on a case-by-case basis.

809 UN Plaza, NY, NY 10017, TEL 212-984-5472, FAX 212-984-5401, SRF@iie.org, www.iie.org/SRF/home

4. The fellowship is to be awarded in the amount of up to US $5,000. The final amount of your fellowship will be based on the location of the host institution, the cost of living, and the value of any financial contributions from the host institution or other source.

5. Fellowship monies may not be transmitted to individuals. They must be sent to the host institution. In order to process the award and transfer the fellowship monies, the Fund requires written agreement from the host university, college or other institution including (i) a statement indicating that the institution agrees to receive the fellowship funds for your support and will act as disbursing agent to you, including arrangements for appropriate visa status, if required, and assuming all responsibilities associated with local, national and international taxation requirements relative to all aspects of the fellowship; (ii) confirmation of the financial or other support to be provided by the institution, and (iii) a name, address, and account to which we should transmit the fellowship funds.

6. You are expected to submit at the end of the fellowship period a brief letter outlining your activities during the fellowship, including any teaching, research or publications undertaken. You are requested to acknowledge the support of the Fund in any publications prepared or published during the fellowship period. The host institution is expected to submit at the end of the fellowship period a brief letter outlining your activities during the fellowship and evaluating the visit. (These letters are important to maintaining financial backing for and improving the operation of the Fund's fellowship activities.)

Please confirm for us as soon as possible that you have received this letter and understand the conditions of the fellowship. We may then begin working with you to arrange for the beginning of your fellowship. You may contact us at +1-212-984-5588 (tel), +1-212

On December 17th 2004 I received a Provisional Admission Letter to do a Full-time Master's degree in Peace and Governance at the Africa University of Mutare, Zimbabwe and in 2005 invited for a workshop on conflict at the United Nations.

AFRICA UNIVERSITY

REGISTRAR'S OFFICE

A UNITED METHODIST - RELATED INSTITUTION

P.O. BOX 1320, MUTARE, ZIMBABWE - TEL: (263-20) 60075/60026/61611/61618 - FAX: (263-20) 61785/66783 - E-MAIL: registrar@africau.ac.zw

December 17, 2004

Mr. George Esambe Ngwane
Executive Director
Africaphonie
Box 364, BUEA
Fako Division, S.W.P
CAMEROON

Dear Mr. G.E. Ngwane

RE: **PROVISIONAL ADMISSION TO AFRICA UNIVERSITY INTO THE INSTITUTE OF PEACE, LEADERSHIP AND GOVERNANCE**

Congratulations!

Your application for entry into the Full-time Masters degree in Peace and Governance (MPG) programme at Africa University has been processed and it is my great pleasure to inform you that you have been granted **provisional admission** into this programme.

To accept this provisional offer of admission and to confirm your intention to study at Africa University, you must now take the following steps IMMEDIATELY:

Step 1. **Acceptance of Admission**

Endorse the attached Acceptance Form of Offer of Admission and return to the Assistant Registrar, Academic Affairs.

Step 2. **Prepayment of University Fees**

All first semester fees must be paid upfront on or before 13 January 2005.

You should now proceed to pay your fees immediately to Africa University through:

The Bursar
Africa University
Box 1320
Mutare
ZIMBABWE

Attached is the **fee structure** for 2004/2005 academic year. The following fees are **directly** payable to the University Bursar:
Tuition
Health
Student Union
Registration
Accommodation (only if you intend to stay in University hostels)

I urge NGOs with an interest in conflict prevention to organize an international conference of local, national and international NGOs on their role in conflict prevention and future interaction with the United Nations in this field. [Report of the UN Secretary-General on the Prevention of Armed conflict, Recommendation 27 (June 2001)]

Utrecht, 7 June2005 Dear Ngwane George,

The Global Partnership for the Prevention of Armed Conflict is pleased that you have accepted our invitation to play an important role in the Global Conference: *From Reaction to Prevention: Civil Society Forging Partnerships to Prevent Violent Conflict and Build Peace*, to be held at the United Nations Headquarters in New York on **19-21 July 2005**. The Global Conference is the culmination of fifteen regional processes, each of which has involved research, discussion, network building, and the organizing of regional conferences. The outcome of these processes includes Regional Action Agendas. The Global Action Agenda has emerged from these regional action agendas and reflects the themes, priorities and recommendations identified in the regional agendas. At the opening session of Conference, the Global Action Agenda will be presented to UN Secretary-General Kofi Annan. During the Conference participants will be encouraged to collectively create implementation plans for the Global Action Agenda, and it is hoped that the time spent working together will bring about initiatives and partnerships between the participants. The Conference participants come from diverse professional backgrounds, including representatives of the UN, governments, regional organizations, as well as civil society representatives.

You will be co-organizing the workshop on 'Indigenous and Local Approaches to Working with Conflict Peacefully', which will take place on Tuesday the 19th July 2005 from 2:30-5:45. Furthermore, we would like to inform you that the European Centre for Conflict Prevention, as the International Secretariat for the Global Conference, will cover your travel costs, your accommodation (we will not cover additional hotel charges of any kind), for the days you are required to be present in New York and 40 USD per diem to cover food, drinks and travel within Manhattan. Travel costs include an economy-class ticket to New York, as well as travel to and from the airport; please note that our budget are currently predicated on low-cost air travel, and we would greatly appreciate if you could endeavor to secure as reasonably-priced airfare as possible. After making the reservation, please send travel and price details to ECCP for approval.

In order to finalize some of these preparations, it would be extremely helpful if we could be informed of your arrival and departure times as soon as possible, so that we may book your accommodation. Also, if you need a visa for travel to the US, and require a special letter of invitation for this, please let us know ASAP, as US visa processes are lengthy.

The Global Conference promises to be an exceptional opportunity to create valuable and lasting change in the fields of peace-building and conflict prevention, and we look forward to working with you in the pursuit of these worthy goals. If you have any questions about your participation in the conference, please do not hesitate to contact me.

Sincerely, on behalf of the Global Partnership for the Prevention of Armed Conflict,

Marte Hellema

Contact Regional Initiators

Central and Eastern Africa
Nairobi Peace Initiative-Africa
Email: fmponyo@npi-africa.org

Southern Africa
The African Centre for the Constructive Resolution of Disputes
Email: renton@accord.org.za

West Africa
West Africa Network for Peacebuilding
Email: ekombande@wanep.org

Latin America and the Caribbean
Regional Coordination for Economic and Social Research
Email: serrakeler@fibertel.com.ar and info@cries.org

North America
Canadian Peacebuilding Coordinating Committee
Email: cpcc@web.ca

InterAction
Email: gppac@interaction.org

South Asia
Regional Centre for Strategic Studies
Email: adrcss@sri lanka.net

The Pacific
Citizens Constitutional Forum
Email: jiokanoa@ccf.org.fj

Southeast Asia
Initiatives for International Dialogue
Email: gus@iidnet.org

Northeast Asia
Peace Boat
Email: gppac@peaceboat.gr.jp

Central Asia
Foundation for Tolerance International
Email: Fti@infotel.kg

Middle East and North Africa
European Centre for Conflict Prevention
Email: bvanhoeven@conflict-prevention.net

Western Commonwealth of Independent States
Nonviolence International
Email: akonenshikov@mail.ru

The Caucasus
International Center on Conflict & Negotiation
Email: iccn@iccn.ge

The Balkans
Nansen Dialogue Network
Email: nansen@eunet.yu

Northern and Western Europe
European Centre for Conflict Prevention
Email: info@conflict-prevention.net

International Secretariat
Global Partnership
for the Prevention of
Armed Conflict
c/o ECCP
P.O. Box 14069
3508 SC Utrecht
The Netherlands
tel. +31-30-242 7777
fax +31-30-236 9268
info@conflict-prevention.net

For some personal reasons, I did not take the Fellowship offer by Scholar Rescue Fund. I did not also travel to New York for the Workshop Invitation by the Global Partnership for the Prevention of Armed Conflict (GPPAC) because of visa problems from U.S Embassy in Cameroon. So I spent 2004, 2005, 2006 and 2007serving an administrative suspension which by Civil service law as shown below should not take more than four months.

Decree No. 94/199 of 7th October 1994 as amended and supplemented by Decree No. 2000/287 of 12th October 2000 to govern the Public Service Rules and Regulations, Section V captioned "SUSPENSION FROM DUTY "reads as follows:

ARTICLE 108 (1) in the event of a serious offence by a civil servant relating to a breach of professional duty, an ordinary law offence or breach of professional ethics, the author of such offence may provisionally be suspended from his duties for not more than FOUR months by the Minister under whom he is serving. The latter shall forthwith inform the Minister in charge of Public Service and forward to him a disciplinary file made in respect of the accused within a period not exceeding one month.

(2) Suspension from duty is a measure of conservation which produces a definitive effect only after a sanction has been taken by competent authority. The civil servant concerned shall stop coming to work during the period of suspension.

(3) If no decision has been taken at the expiry of the period referred to in (1) above, the suspended civil servant shall automatically resume his post.

I turned down suggestions by lawyers to press charges against the government. Anyone familiar with the modus operandus of our judicial and executive marriage would understand why and anyone who can decipher that my sanction was political than professional would understand why.

On 7th September 2007 a new Minister of Culture in the name of Madam Ama Tutu Muna was appointed and I thought this was a window of opportunity to present my suspension case anew. I wrote this letter to her on 11th September 2007.

Fax: 2222 6579

11th September 2007

H. E. Madam Ama Tutu Muna
Minister of Culture
Yaounde
Her Excellency,

Subject: CONGRATULATIONS and SUSPENSION as Provincial Delegate for Culture for the South West Province

I am Mr Ngwane George Esambe; Provincial Delegate for Culture for the South West Province, appointed on March 5th 2004 then suspended 4 months later (5th July 2004).

Since then my situation has not been regularised and I am still (for 3 years now) serving my suspension sentence as Provincial Delegate in the Delegation of Culture in the South West Province.

Her Excellency, I wish to extend to you my warmest congratulations as the new Minister for Culture.

Her Excellency, I would appreciate if you grant me audience to discuss with you my present situation as suspended Provincial Delegate for Culture for the South West Province.

Yours sincerely,

Ngwane George Esambe
Tel: 77 66 84 79
Fax: 33 32 25 43

I then invited myself for an audience with the Minister who received me so warmly, showed sympathy for my situation and requested the Secretary General to prepare a document for my reinstatement as Delegate. I waited for another year and decided to invite myself for another audience with the Minister but this time she refused granting the audience and instead asked me to see her Technical Adviser Dr Madam Asheri Kilo. Madam Kilo did not understand why I had been sent to see her. I now understood what my late friend Ateba Eyene Charles told me when I met with him on the stairs of the Ministry of Culture the second time I came to see the Minister. Charles who was also under controversial status in the Ministry advised me not to bother seeing the Minister because he (Charles) and I had been blacklisted in the Ministry as "rebellious writers". Otherwise how could one explain the hospitable reception during my first audience and the lukewarm reception later on? Finally after spending another year under the new Minister as a "Delegate on suspension" and with Mr Roger Lita acting as interim Delegate for four years I got replaced on 14th November 2008 by Mr Nyobe … "as Delegate for Culture for South West Province". With this formal replacement I knew my future in the Ministry of Culture was bleak but I was advised to stick on. I therefore needed an Assumption of Duty. I went to the Ministry of Culture in Yaounde for an assumption of Duty on 19th November 2008 but the Secretary General of the Ministry asked me to return two weeks later as the Ministry was busy with preparations of the National Festival of Arts and Culture. I came back on 8th January 2009, 9th March 2009, and 16th March 2009 but there was no Assumption of Duty for me. Then on 19th March 2009 the Minister came out with fresh appointments and as can be seen on this Appointment Decision placing me under the Department of Cultural Patrimony in the Ministry of Culture in Yaounde, I was the only one whose Civil Service Registration Number was not on the Appointment Decision.

REPUBLIQUE DU CAMEROUN
Paix-travail-Patrie

MINISTERE DE LA CULTURE

DIRECTION DES AFFAIRES GENERALES

SERVICE DU PERSONNEL

REPUBLIC OF CAMEROON
Peace-Work-Fatherland

MINISTRY OF CULTURE

NOTE N° 007 MINCULT / DAG / SP
Portant affectation de certains Cadres en service au Ministère de la Culture.

A compter de la date de signature de la présente note, les cadres ci-après désignés en service au Ministère de la Culture reçoivent les affectations suivantes :

- **Secrétariat Général : Cellule de Traduction :**
  Monsieur AHMADOU MOHAMAN, Mle 546 405-0, Traducteur Principal.

- **Direction des Arts, Spectacles et Entreprises culturelles :**
  Monsieur TONYE Michel Archange, Mle 166342-E, Cadre Contractuel d'Administration.

- **Direction des Archives :**
  Monsieur ATEBA Simon Davy, Mle 540216-R, Conseiller Principal de Jeunesse et d'Animation.

- **Direction du Patrimoine Culturel :**
  Monsieur NGWANE Georges ESAMBE, Professeur des Lycées d'Enseignement Général.

La présente Note d'affectation sera enregistrée et communiquée partout où besoin sera.

Yaoundé, le 19 MAR. 2009

Ampliations :

- MINCULT/SG/SC
- MINCULT/DAG/SP
- MINCULT/D.A
- MINCULT/DPC
- Intéressés/ Chrono/Archives.

I resumed as Staff in the Department of Cultural Patrimony on 20 April 2009 and was given a Certificate of Assumption of Duty.

REPUBLIQUE DU CAMEROUN Paix – Travail – Patrie ---------- **MINISTERE DE LA CULTURE** --------- **SECRETARIAT GENERAL** --------- **DIRECTION DU PATRIMOINE CULTUREL** ---------	**REPUBLIC OF CAMEROON** Peace – Work – Fatherland ---------- **MINISTRY OF CULTURE** ---------- **SECRETARIAT GENERAL** ---------- **DEPARTMENT OF CULTURAL HERITAGE** ----------

N° 0001/Mincult/DPC

20 AVR 2009

CERTIFICAT DE PRISE DE SERVICE

Je soussigné Directeur du Patrimoine Culturel, certifie que Monsieur NGWANE Georges ESAMBE, Professeur des Lycées d'Enseignement Général, précédemment Délégué Provincial de la Culture du Sud-Ouest (Buea) Mle 353 483 A affecté par Note de Service N° 007/MINCULT/DAG.SP du 19 mars 2009 a effectivement pris son service à la Direction du Patrimoine Culturel du Ministère de la Culture.

En foi de quoi la présente attestation lui est établie pour servir et valoir ce que de droit.

Directeur du Patrimoine Culturel

Marthe Dorisca Madou

The same day of 20th April 2009, I asked my Director of Cultural Patrimony Madam Marthe Darisca Medou to show me my office and spell out my duties. She first of all apologized for lack of office space and hoped I would not mind sitting in her secretariat. As for my duties, there was nothing specific but I should be on hand for any assignment she would devolve to me when need arose. The following day she gave me an assignment to translate UNESCO documents from English language –a language which she did not master very well to French language – a language whose technical jargon I did not master. I knew then that I was in the wrong place. Even office cleaners in the Ministry have an office where they keep their buckets and rags and where they can change from their house dresses to work attire. Even office cleaners have a specific term of work assignment which is one of cleaning an office. And here was Ngwane without an office and without any job specification. Here was Ngwane who had his first Assumption of Duty in the Public Service as pioneer English language Teacher of Government Secondary Diang (East Region) on 8th November 1983 (twenty-six years after) being told to sit idly in a Director's secretariat until she leaves her office. Ngwane as a teacher then a Senior Discipline Master, then Vice Principal, then functional Delegate of Culture for four months was in search of a working environment in the name of an office. I know that public service life is full of fluctuating fortunes with some enjoying all the perks and privileges of life in the beginning and as we are now seeing in Cameroon ending in the confines of prison cells. Indeed for some, public service life can be a paradise from the beginning to the end while for others a quintessential stations of the cross. If mine was the quintessential Stations of the Cross, then my appointment into the Department of Cultural Patrimony was the tenth station of the cross and I had no desire to wait till I reach the twelfth station. No, not at the December of my civil service career. I spent only three days in the Department of Cultural Patrimony and on 22 April 2009, I wrote this letter to the Minister of Culture and left back for Buea.

Of course there was no reply hence urging me to write a second letter on 14th July 2009

Department of Cultural Heritage
Ministry of Culture
Yaounde
22 April 2009

The Minister of Culture
Yaounde

Her Excellency,

Subject: Return to my Ministry of origin: Ministry of Secondary Education

I, Ngwane George Esambe, recently transferred by Note 007/ MINCULT/ DAG/ SP of 19 March 2009, to the Department of Cultural Heritage, Ministry of Culture, Yaounde, wish to be redeployed to my Ministry of origin- Ministry of Secondary Education.

Ngwane George Esambe
PLEG
Matricule No. 3535483-A

Then finally I got what I requested for as shown through this Decision by the Minister of Culture

REPUBLIQUE DU CAMEROUN
Paix-Travail-Patrie
MINISTERE DE LA CULTURE
SECRETARIAT GENERAL
DIRECTION DES AFFAIRES GENERALES
SERVICE DU PERSONNEL
N°1874/MINCULT/SG/DAG/SP/

REPUBLIC OF CAMEROON
Peace-Work-Fatherland
MINISTRY OF CULTURE

Yaoundé, le 13 OCT 2009

Le Ministre De La Culture

A

Monsieur Le Ministre des Enseignements Secondaires
- YAOUNDE -

Objet : Remise à disposition de Monsieur NGWANE George ESSAMBE

J'ai l'honneur de remettre à la disposition de votre Département ministériel et à sa demande le personnel nommé en objet jusqu'alors en service à la Direction du Patrimoine Culturel au Ministère de la Culture. /.

Ama Tutu Muna

The next month and precisely on 2 November 2009, the British High Commission Cameroon sent me this letter offering me a Foreign and Commonwealth Office Chevening Fellowship Award to study Conflict Prevention and Resolution course at the University of York (UK) for 4 months.

On my return from the Chevening Fellowship from the UK, I was sent as auxiliary staff to the Delegation of Secondary Education in Buea, South West Region and finally to the Government High School Buea Rural as one of the School Librarians.

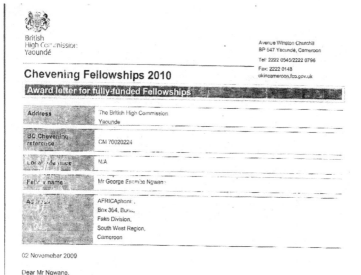

British
High Commission
Yaoundé

Avenue Winston Churchill
BP 547 Yaoundé, Cameroon
Tel: 2222 0545/2222 0796
Fax: 2222 0148
ukincameroon.fco.gov.uk

Chevening Fellowships 2010

Award letter for fully-funded Fellowships

Address	The British High Commission Yaounde
BC Chevening reference	CM 70020224
Local reference	N/A
Fellow name	Mr George Essambe Ngwane
Address	AFRICAphone, Box 364, Buea, Fako Division, South West Region, Cameroon

02 Novemeber 2009

Dear Mr Ngwane,

I have pleasure in offering you a Foreign & Commonwealth Office (FCO) Chevening Fellowship Award to study on the Conflict Prevention & Resolution course at the University of York. Your FCO Chevening Fellowship will start on Saturday 9 January 2010 (flying Friday 8 January if flight is not available on Saturday 9 January) and will end on Thursday 1 April 2010. You are required to adhere to these dates precisely.

This letter and information pack contain important information which you must read now. The British Council will contact you shortly to help you make arrangements to travel to the United Kingdom.

Once the letter is signed by you, the documents in the pack will constitute a contract between you and the British Council and will be governed by English law.

The documents are:

- Acceptance Form
- Health Information and Declaration
- The Chevening website and terms and conditions of use
- Frequently Asked Questions (FAQs). Please visit www.Chevening.com and select your course for this information in the members area
- Visa information & supporting letters (Please ask the British Council and British Embassy/British High Commission to provide these)

In October 2014 I was selected and offered a Rotary Peace Fellowship to study three months of Conflict Resolution in the University of Chulalongkorn, Bangkok, Thailand.

Rotary

10 October 2014

Dear George Ngwane:

On behalf of the Trustees of The Rotary Foundation, we are pleased to inform you that you have been selected to receive a 2015 Rotary Peace Fellowship for studies as part of the Rotary Peace Centers. You have been assigned to the Rotary Peace Center at Chulalongkorn University in Bangkok, Thailand, to attend the winter session, which will occur 7 January – 27 March 2015.

Because of the limited size of each session, The Rotary Foundation will not consider requests for transfer to a different session ***except*** in cases of emergency. If you do not wish to study in the session to which you are assigned, you will forfeit your seat in the program.

This e-mail contains your acceptance packet which has comprehensive information about the program, including *A Guide to Your Rotary Peace Fellowship.* Your primary contact at The Rotary Foundation will be Emily Ruf, Rotary Peace Centers Specialist. If your mailing or email address changes, please notify her immediately at:

Emily.Ruf@rotary.org
phone: +1-847-866-3252

The Rotary Foundation and our university partner considered candidates from all over the world for the Rotary Peace Fellowships in a highly competitive selection process. You should feel proud of this significant achievement. The Rotary Foundation looks forward to a lifelong relationship with you.

Sincerely,

Kathleen O'Brien
Rotary Peace Centers Relationship Supervisor
The Rotary Foundation

Enclosures

cc: Governor, 9150, RI
Rotary Foundation Chair, 9150, RI
Rotary Peace Fellow Chair, 9150, RI
Sponsor Counselor, RI
Club President, RI
Rotary Peace Center Director, Chulalongkorn University
Host Area Coordinator, Chulalongkorn University, RI

ONE ROTARY CENTER 1560 SHERMAN AVENUE EVANSTON, ILLINOIS 60201-3698 USA · WWW.ROTARY.ORG

In December 2015, I was once again selected and offered a Commonwealth Professional Development Fellowship as a mid-career agent to study and exchange service knowledge on minority issues tenable with Minority Rights International Group London for three months (February-April 2016).

Commonwealth Scholarship
Commission in the UK

Woburn House
20-24 Tavistock Square
London WC1H 9HF
United Kingdom

T +44 (0)20 7380 6700
F +44 (0)20 7387 2655
www.dfid.gov.uk/cscuk

Mr. George Esambe Ngwane
Box 384 Buea, Fako Division South West
Region, Cameroon
Cameroon

17/12/2015
CMCP-2015-212

Dear Mr. Ngwane

Confirmation of Award

Thank you for returning the award acceptance form for our offer of a Commonwealth Professional Fellowship tenable at **Minority Rights Group International**. As you have now met all conditions expressed in our Notification of Award, I am able to confirm the Commission's offer of a Fellowship.

By becoming a Commonwealth Fellow in the United Kingdom, you are following in a tradition of over 22,000 individuals holding Commonwealth Awards since the scheme began over fifty years ago. You can find out more about the Commonwealth Scholarship and Fellowship Plan, including the names of previous award holders, by visiting our web site at: www.dfid.gov.uk/cscuk. Your Commonwealth Fellowship is funded by the UK *Department for International Development* (DFID). DFID supports our work as part of its strategy to develop people and skills that will contribute directly to the development of their countries.

During and after your award, we will also ask you at various times for information about your progress, and what impact your award has had. Please make the most of these opportunities, and reply to such requests promptly. Please help us to publicise the scheme, too, by describing yourself as a 'Commonwealth Professional Fellow' wherever possible. The more evidence and ambassadors that we have for the scheme, the stronger our case for ensuring that it continues to receive support.

We're keen that you become involved in the Commonwealth Scholarship and Fellowship community as quickly as possible; included with this confirmation is the information on our online and regional networks as well as details of how to keep up to date with our events.

I look forward to your coming to take up this award.

Yours sincerely

JOHN KIRKLAND
Executive Secretary

COMMONWEALTH
SCHOLARSHIPS

On 4th July 2016, I was selected to participate in the one month November 2016 Minorities Fellowship Programme at the Office of the High Commissioner for Human Rights in Geneva, Switzerland.

NATIONS UNIES
DROITS DE L'HOMME
HAUT-COMMISSARIAT

UNITED NATIONS
HUMAN RIGHTS
OFFICE OF THE HIGH COMMISSIONER

HAUT-COMMISSARIAT AUX DROITS DE L'HOMME • OFFICE OF THE HIGH COMMISSIONER FOR HUMAN RIGHTS
PALAIS DES NATIONS • 1211 GENEVA 10, SWITZERLAND
www.ohchr.org • TEL: +41 22 917 9000 • FAX: +41 22 917 9008 • E-MAIL: registry@ohchr.org

Geneva, 4 July 2016

Dear Mr. Ngwane,

I have the pleasure to inform you that you have been selected to participate in the 2016 Minorities Fellowship Programme at the Office of the High Commissioner for Human Rights in Geneva, Switzerland.

The objective of this programme is to give you the opportunity to gain knowledge on the UN system and mechanisms, dealing particularly with minority issues, so you can better assist in protecting and promoting the rights of persons belonging to minorities and disseminate the knowledge acquired. We sincerely hope that you will take this opportunity as a commitment towards your community and that our Office will also benefit from your valuable contribution.

The Minorities Fellowship Programme will start on Monday 7 November and will end on Friday 25 November 2016. During the Fellowship Programme, you will be entitled to the following:

- An air ticket (economy class) from your country of origin to Geneva and return.
- Basic health insurance for the duration of the Programme.
- A daily stipend of CHF 130 to cover your basic expenses, including accommodation.

Please bear in mind that any other personal expenses, except for those specified above, will be your responsibility.

We would need to receive as soon as possible a written confirmation indicating that you will participate in the 2016 Minorities Fellowship programme and that you accept the conditions set above. Thank you for sending the enclosed confirmation as a scanned copy with your signature by email to brodriguezdealba@ohchr.org. We will be in contact with you concerning practical arrangements once we have received your acceptance.

Please do not hesitate to contact us, should you need further information.

Yours sincerely,

Antti Korkeakivi
Chief,
Indigenous Peoples and Minorities Section

Mr. George Ngwane
e-mail: gngwane@yahoo.com

On my return from these Fellowships, I started reminiscing over my stay in the Ministry of Culture and a possibility of asking for voluntary retirement from the public service. As functional Delegate for Culture of South West, I toured the length and breadth of the South West to create or reorganize the Divisional Cultural Associations; in three months I visited the headquarters of four of the six divisions of the South West to celebrate World Music day, World Museum Day, World Artists' Day and World Book Day consolidating my philosophy that leadership is not about the quantity of years one puts in but the quality of service one gives out. Yet in Cameroonian Administration there is only the voice of the hierarchy that is heard and that to quote the Nigerian Author Chimamanda Ngozi Adichie is the danger of a single story. In Cameroonian administration I am forced to believe that output does not matter as much as blind loyalty by servile flatterers. Dr E.M.L Endeley once said in a political rally in 1965 in the then West Cameroon "Foncha is surrounded by flatterers, political vultures, place seekers and ambitious men who take advantage of Foncha's humility". It is true the day before yesterday as it is today and the day after tomorrow. With all sincere modesty until the arrival of Madam Grace Ngoh as Delegate of Culture in 2014 who is showing remarkable and relative grasp of art and culture vision, I have been so stupefied by the crassness that has captured the Delegation of Culture since I was finally dismissed in 2009 that I wonder whether work ethics has any place in our country. Yes with all sincere modesty I challenge the Ministry of Culture through its Delegation in the South West to show me the milestones or benchmarks of succeeding Delegates since I was shown the door in 2009 because of my writings. And I still stand by the relevance and resonance of my writings. Dr Bernard Fonlon while serving as Deputy Minister of Foreign affairs and Federal Member of Parliament for Nso constituency observed that his writings had very often been misrepresented by certain people and explained in ways to twist his original intention. He was therefore obliged to write a serialized treatise in Cameroon Times newspaper on the Tuesday December 14th 1965 edition under the caption "The Task today" in which he wrote inter alia "The acts of government are not right merely because it is invested with authority. There is a test by which they must be tried, a purpose towards which they must tend. That is the fundamental reason why the citizen has the right and the duty of scrutinizing both the motive and the character of government acts. The government therefore like the ordinary citizen is bound to answer for its action. This is what we mean fundamentally when we talk of the Rule of Law. Without the Rule of Law, there is either tyranny or chaos".

As a Delegate I probably was wrong into believing that the Delegation's budget was meant for carrying out activities in Art and Culture and for artists and their associations. I must have been deluded into believing that state resources were meant for development architecture and not for stomach infrastructure. I must have been wrong into believing that appointments were about service not status, performance not privileges and projects not promises. Yet until we as a Cameroonian people revolutionise our Mentality Adjustment Program and stop making scholars soft target for our political ineptitude, we shall continue to live in a country in motion without movement and in a country with all the human and natural capital whose citizens are still stuck in the mire of crass inertia and cushioned mediocrity. There are legions of examples of persons both in the secular and even in God's Ministry who have been victimized for their beliefs and values and the consequence is that human resources are being sacrificed on the altar of economic growth. For a country that has the ambition to recapture her lost middle income status, for a country that boasts of a huge critical mass of human capital, for a country that has all the potentials of a double digit economic development, political patronage and intolerance to creative freedom must be anathema.

After being released to my Ministry of origin which is the Ministry of Education in the South West Region, I now have the pleasure as my retirement in the civil service looms around, and as of the time of completing this Diary in 2016, to serve as School Librarian of Government High School, Buea Rural. My major achievements there so far have been sourcing for books from Book aid International London, converting the library inventory from manual to electronic and above all organizing a library workshop for School librarians in Fako Division on 23rd April 2013 (World Book Day)

Yet I still believe in the power in the writer (title of one of my books) or to paraphrase Ngugi wa Thiong'o the barrel of the pen. I believe in Socrates the writer-philosopher who spared no pains in urging the city's rulers towards goodness, truth and justice. When Socrates was accused of and arraigned to court for being a menace to society because of his writings, he told the court "Gentlemen, you know that I am not going to alter my conduct not even if I have to die a hundred deaths. If you put me to death, you will not easily find anyone to take my place. I suspect however that before long you will awake from your drowsing and in annoyance, you will take Anytus' advice and finish me off with a single slap; and then you will go on sleeping till the end of your days, unless God in his care for you sends someone to take my place". After twenty-five years of newspaper writings I decided to stop writing for newspapers in 2015 (have I?),even though God in his care for Cameroon has sent others to take the places of Bate Besong, Dibussi Tande, Churchill Monono, Bob Forbin, Ntemfac Ofege, Boh Herbert, Julius Wamey, Paddy Mbawa, Adolf Dipoko, Jing Thomas Ayeah, Charles Taku, Tina Nganda, Charly Wirsuiy,Peter Vakunta, Barry Fortung, Rodcod Gobata, Sam Nuvala Fonkem, Francis Wache, Hilary Kebila Fokum, Cyprian Agbor, Atem Ebini, Chief Etah Besong, Chief Nzoh Ngandembou, Charlie Ndi Chi, Martin Jumbam, Zama Ndefru and Ngwane in reawakening the consciousness of Cameroonians and to democratic and liberal values, as attested by this article written by one among the new generation of young Turks Macdonald Ayang:

"My pen, my pain and my pleasure" ***Mwalimu George Ngwane***

By Macdonald Ayang Okumb ***in the Eden newspaper of October 2012***

After having written what he called his last newspaper feature titled "In dire need of Anglophone media moguls" which was published in some English language newspapers, civil society activist and Executive Director of a Non-Governmental Organisation, AFRICAphonie, Mwalimu George Ngwane, has shared with Eden some of the hallmarks of his 25 years writing career.

"After the last article, I have had some feedback, people wondering whether that was my farewell feature-writing. Yes it is. It's been real wonderful because I have been writing since 1987" he said.

The Mwalimu also quickly recalled some of those bitter days when he used his pen; "…I then knew the power of the pen in 1990 when I wrote and was arrested and detained for two weeks while I was just a teacher in Government High School Mundemba. That's when I knew that the pen actually was mightier than the sword even though it is said that the sword is mightier than the holder of the pen. Subsequently when I wrote an article in 2004 on Cameroon democracy, I was suspended and eventually dismissed as Delegate of Culture. Those were the watershed years for me when it comes to how much writing can impact on national life. I picked especially on the democratic process of Cameroon, the Vision 2020 on which I wrote which caused me my job. Later on, they started talking about the Vision 2035 which seems to be the sing song that the CPDM government uses for Cameroon to become a middle income country."

To him, his writing was very much in context; "But if you look at the various writings, they have a context. We wrote, and I am using 'we' because they were a lot of us who wrote at the time what we called liberation writing and what we wrote in the

1990s was basically on the Anglophone struggle. In the 2000s, we started looking into how well we were into this union."

"…quite recently, I went back again to my Anglophone soul which to me represents my wellbeing and my all. And one of the articles that struck me, and for which I also got feedback, was titled "once upon a time Buea; Articles that are nostalgic, articles that give one a feeling of a sense of loss. These articles actually seem to impact a lot in the lives of people…"

According to Ngwane, writing is not just an art; "I wrote just recently on Anglophones and the media. I am extremely disappointed with what I call the Anglophone solidarity. Writing to me is not an art; it's a policy advocacy tool. Writing to me makes sense if what I write can help formulate or change certain policies. It doesn't make sense to me when people meet me on the way and say I love your writing, until what I write is translated into what I call policy engagement or policy influence."

As to whether his decision to quit newspaper writing didn't come at a time he should have even done more, he responded thus; "…I am 50 and the last man standing. Most of Those with whom I wrote in the 1990s such as Dibussi Tande have either gone abroad or just kept their silence. When I looked at the newspaper pages, it looked like I was the only one still writing of the 1990 generation. And when I look at young people whose writings I actually enjoy reading, I say ah! May be, it's time for me to pass the relay baton to another generation. I hope this generation shall focus on public and human interest feature writing rather than personality cult, hero-worshipping and ego-massaging narratives, all for a fee.

But that doesn't mean I have opted out of writing as it were. I have a website www.gngwane.com and I still post most of my articles on my website. But I still think that it's time to let another generation say its own story, having said mine."

Having experienced the world of civil service, of scholarly astuteness, of knowledge production and of civil society, I am not surprised that a former Deputy Governor of Lagos state in

Nigeria disclosed in a popular Talk show "Teju Baby Face Show" that her initial intention was to be a business person rather than a Deputy Governor. She accepted the latter more as a call to service. That is why most countries that provide an enabling climate for private sector growth, blossom more than those that see the private sector as rivals or threats. Countries that give free reign to private sector competition rather than state control over citizens' opportunities rank high in the human development index. Non-state actors, independent thinkers and the private sector are indispensable partners in our nation's drive to greater vision and mission. The civil society's contribution to nation building remains enormous yet underutilized. Life is about choices and the choices we make inadvertently affect our success stories. Success can be measured by philosophical depths or material heights. Success depends on who you are competing with, what your objectives and goals are and what personal satisfaction you derive from it. Yet there is no fiercer competitor of yours than you. So life is about following your instincts and never allowing closed doors to blur your vision towards open windows. Before my unpleasant encounter in the Ministry of Culture, I had had real satisfaction in the Ministry of Education. For close to twenty-one years as a teacher in secondary schools, the Ministry had provided me with life's opportunities but the writer in me has provided me with a personal epiphany. On 27th July 2015, while in Yaounde, I bumped into Bob Forbin one of Cameroon's erstwhile Publishers and Editor of the household newspaper called "The Herald". I asked why with all the success he had recorded as a Publisher he decided to fold up business after training a battery of journalists some of whom have their own media organs today. He told me he had spent so much time working for others and now he had decided to introspect and find his inner voice. That inner voice has been speaking volumes of messages with his persona which now resonates with a peace with himself and a communication link with his deity. He forwarded a 537 page book called "In the light of Truth" through the internet. I have read every page of it and understand now that life indeed is about knowing when to separate the moon from the stars. On page 16 of the book are the following words "Thus make yourselves independent, burst the fetters that hold you down! If obstacles present themselves, welcome them joyfully, for they mean you are on the right way to freedom and spiritual power. Look on them as gifts by which you can profit and then you will overcome them with ease. They are either put on your way to teach and to mature you, or maybe, they are the result of some debt you have incurred which you can settle in this way and free yourself. In either they will help your advance. Set out to meet them with a bold heart-it is for your own good."

I know so many people who have had a brush with the civil service and have become transformers of lives in the private sector. I hope one day they will tell us their story. So are there transformers of sustainable livelihoods among those who are still parading the corridors of civil service in Cameroon. I hope they shall muster time, courage and resources someday to tell us their narrative. Only you can best tell your own story for indeed like Chinua Achebe said until the lion becomes its own historian, the story of the hunt shall always glorify the hunter.

I became more conscious of my role as a secondary school teacher (Mwalimu) cum School Administrator and its impact on my former students when I travelled to Bangkok, Thailand for the 3 month course on Peace and Conflict studies at the University of Chulalongkorn in 2015. Taking advantage of the smooth, free and speedy internet connectivity in Bangkok, I re-opened my Facebook account and in less than two weeks my Facebook messages were inundated with highly positive compliments from my former students. I felt the impact I had made on human resources and closed my eyes in praise to God's divine power and grace. For the record, I did not turn to civil society practice because of the misadventure I had with the Ministry of Culture. For the record, the Ministry of Arts and Culture especially under the tutelage of Madam Ama Tutu Muna had become the mortuary of civil servants of South West stock as no South Westerner was Regional Delegate during my suspension, Wang Johnson was dismissed as Director of Cinematography, Professor Paul Ndue who replaced him was obliged to withdraw to the University and Mr Herbert Ediage who was Director of Administration and Finance was kicked out. As far back as in the early 90s when I was posted to Bilingual Grammar School Buea from Government High School Mundemba I met civil society gurus like Shey Benjy Serkfem, Charlie Mbonteh, Tabot Ebenezer Tabot, George Bejuka, Ndumbe Nkumbe, Jerome Gwellem, Anu Vincent, Clarkson Obasi, Chief Nzoh Ngandembou, Moses Tabe, Louis Nkembi etc. who fired the compulsion in me to found the civil society organisations AFRICAphonie on 30th November 1998 and the National Book Development Council in 1999. Since then I have always been a citizen of these two spaces knowing how complementary they are and deriving intellectual and social reward from both. But truth must be said that my ultimate fulfilment as a civil servant was torpedoed and brought to question by my short stint in the Ministry of Culture. Without family, friends and even foes who hailed and nailed my resolve to forge ahead I probably would have been telling another tale. Paradoxically it was this triangular club of family, friends and foes that triggered me to appreciate the Grail of civil society professionalism and the luxury of unfettered intellectual freedom. And so with just some light years ahead of my retirement in the civil service, I look back and thank the Ministry of Education for providing me a monthly salary and subsequently periodic pension allowance; but I look ahead and thank the civil society even with its own fair share of intrigues, blackmail, undercutting, donor fatigue, intellectual project proposal challenges and impotent advocacy impact, for making me Independent and assertive. As civil society actor and public intellectual, I have had the opportunity to be invited to mentor young people about career and life skills. My sound bite to them is "never, never allow someone else define you; never, never allow someone to tell you, you are dead simply because you are asleep"

On 11th July 2014, I was invited 'as a Resource person and role model for young people' by the General Manager of the National Civic Service Agency for the participation in Development to make a presentation to some 400 conscripts aged between 17 and 21 years. My presentation was summarised in11 core values on life's lessons:

1) Carve out a niche for yourself by using your talent wisely and exhibiting positive values of your personality and your character.

2) Always under promise and over deliver. This can be done by taking up assignments you are sure to complete, beating deadlines and being reliable.

3) Often make a checklist of your calendar of activities weekly, monthly and annually with room for flexibility

4) Be committed in whatever passion or career you undertake

5) Manage your energy (physical, mental, emotional and spiritual) judiciously

6) Man or woman, know and be thyself, for this will let your right attitude take you to the highest altitude

7) Keep in mind the canons of corporate culture (appropriate dress code, decent language ethics, good human relations, and a good mix of character, chemistry and creativity).

8) Follow your instincts while keeping an ear to public opinion

9) Remember that in Africa it takes a community to raise a child so always try to give back to your community. Cameroon has a fertile recipe for human capital export. In fact to quote Issa Tchiroma when he was at his best as Opposition leader in a 2010 interview in the Eden newspaper "if the country was properly managed, youths wouldn't leave to other countries. We are to blame. In the 60s ,70s and 80s, Cameroonians were proud of their country and youths did not migrate. Let's build our

economy and give the youths better chances and they will not leave the country."

10) Even with all the frustrations, failure and fatigue in life, if you cannot be the fastest to cross the finishing line, keep on keeping on for like the Americans are wont to say "it is never over until it is over".

11) Live by the ideals of a pan African youth by believing in GLOCALISATION (thinking Global and acting local) or what Tony Elumelu calls Africapitalism, Julius Nyerere calls Ujamaa and Afrocentric political economists call autocentric or endogenous thinking rather than the banal and opaque concept of Globalisation.

As a father and husband I tell my family members and those coming for mentorship and coaching that working in the civil service is not the be-all and end-all of life. If they have the culture and nurture to serve the community through the civil service so be it, but let it be with diligence and the penultimate purpose of rendering service to humanity. Career is not about longevity as it is about legacy. As civil society actor and drum major for creative freedom, I have travelled widely in Africa, Europe and Asia; as a civil society actor and apologist of intellectual thinking, I have been invited to coach and mentor on national and international platforms; as civil society actor and votary of truth, I have written articles in numerous newspapers and diverse International journals since 1990 and published more than ten books to date; as civil society actor and crusader for positive peace, I am a Member of the Cultural Policy Task Force in Africa, a member of the Editorial Advisory Board of the African Book Publishing Record, UK, World Wide Fund Scholar (Jordanhill College Glasgow, Scotland 1991), Senior Chevening Peace Fellow (University of York UK 2010), Rotary Peace Fellow (University of Chulalongkorn, Bangkok, Thailand 2015) Commonwealth Professional Fellow (Minority Rights Group International, London UK 2015) and Minorities Rights Fellow (United Nations Human Rights Commission, Geneva,

Switzerland 2016); as civil society actor and advocate for meritocracy, my blog www.gngwane.com was in 2009 selected among the 100 best blogs for learning in Africa, I was awarded best political essayist by the then Cameroon Post newspaper in 1991,was recognized as Commonwealth Personality in 2013 by the Commonwealth Students' Union of the University of Buea in "acknowledging the efforts I have been making towards the upliftment of the commonwealth values and principles in Cameroon" ,my organisation AFRICAphonie was designated 2014 civil society organisation of the Year Award by The Scoop 2014 Excellence Award and in 2015 my blog was shortlisted among the top blogs in Cameroon. I have used my two civil society associations to organise debates on policy advocacy, to engage conversations on sustainable livelihoods and to host events on capacity building with more than 2500 beneficiaries from Buea to Bakassi and from Bamenda to Yaounde as testified by invitations to national forums and especially this article that was an examination question in a public examination in 2012.

REPUBLIC OF CAMEROON
Peace-Work-Fatherland
....
MINESEC/ DECC

CAP INDUSTRIAL
2012 Session
Time allowed: 2 hours
Coefficient: 1

ENGLISH LANGUAGE

AUTHORISED DOCUMENTS
No document is authorised besides those given by the examiner.
N.B. Before you begin, make sure you have been given all the necessary pages.

LISTENING COMPREHENSION /5 marks
(Time allowed: 30 minutes)

Instructions for the conduct of this section of the examination

The passage is to be read twice. The first reading is to be at normal speed without any interruptions while the candidates just listen. Then the question papers are distributed. The passage is read for the second and last time with slight pauses for candidates to take notes if they wish.

THE PROCEDURE FOR GIVING THE LISTENING COMPREHENSION

Reader says:

I am going to read a short passage to you twice before you answer the questions on it. During the first reading, listen attentively to the passage. You are not allowed to write anything during the first reading.

- ***First reading :............***
- ***Teacher distributes question papers.***
- ***Reader says :***

I shall now read the passage for the second and final time. You may look at the questions and may take notes if you wish as I read

Final reading: ....

1/7

REPUBLIC OF CAMEROON
Peace-Work-Fatherland
....
MINESEC/ DECC

CAP INDUSTRIAL
2012...Session
Time allowed: 2 hours
Coefficient : 1

ENGLISH LANGUAGE

AUTHORISED DOCUMENTS
No document is authorised besides those given by the examiner.
N.B. Before you begin, make sure you have been given all the necessary pages.

PAPER I (5 MARKS) *(Time allowed: 30 minutes)*

LISTENING COMPREHENSION - (PASSAGE TO BE READ)

The man of culture, educationist and pan-africanist, Nwalimu George Ngwane, has donated 2.100 volumes of assorted books to some 21 schools in Fako division. The beneficiaries include Primary, Secondary and High schools. The books, as an offer from the International Book Project (IBP), were handed to beneficiaries October 14, 2009. School Principals and Head-Masters, amid student representatives, received the books at the Buea Clerks Quarters' ceremonial ground. On the occasion, Ngwane explained to beneficiaries that the underlying aim was to encourage reading among students, widen their scope of knowledge and equip them with research material.

The gesture added to earlier book donations by the same donors and was applauded by onlookers as a magnificent opening for pupils and students to train themselves in reading zeal. Ngwane said the books covered a variety of topics with the prime objective of improving on library development. He said there was evident repository in the reading culture as well as an absence of school libraries.

"Our gesture is a bridge to take readers to libraries and librarians to readers", Ngwane posited. He observed a lacunae that most school Administrators do not put priority on libraries. Also, they had visited many schools around Buea and noticed a lack and a displaced thought about libraries. In the same vein, he remarked that the few existing libraries around Fako seem to be mere warehouses where books are dumped and very few come to read them. Language proficiency can be built through reading, educationists explain.

By NKEZE MBONWOH.

Culled from Cameroon tribune, November 09, 2009.p.15

2/7

Life is not a linear continuum but an undulating circle of circumstances with its crest and falls. My civil society experience has taught me to rely on myself without being self-centred, to appreciate the extreme warmth of my wife and children without being parochial and to daily open communication lines with God Almighty without being fanatical. My wife always says "Man is a lonely creature" but with a supportive, nuclear and extended family, empathetic and trustworthy friends and a prayerful heart that "loneliness" can be transformed into "loveliness".

My life as a civil society actor and free canon has brought me much closer to community pro-people relations. Yes, the South African Ubuntu philosophy that says "I am because we are" or the biblical precept of being my brother's keeper has been manifested through my family's endeavour to reach out when we can, to the vulnerable, the disadvantaged and those at the base of the economic pyramid. This personal essay is not a travelogue of self-conceit but a compass on how we can all transform our obstacles into opportunities and our blurred visions of doom into our bright vistas of boom. So do all of these preclude me from accepting any appointment in the public service again? Not at all. But such an appointment shall still be steeped in this statement by the virologist, former Commissioner for Education and Special Duties, Rivers State (1975-79), Minister for Petroleum Resources (1978-85) and Minister for Mines, Power and Steel (1985-86) for Nigerian Government, Professor Tamucemi Sokari Tam David-West as he says "an Academic in government must be analytical, unpretentious and give valid solutions to problems. He must speak out against injustice and corruption. He must not allow himself to be emasculated in government. The day he loses his conscience, he ceases to be an intellectual. He becomes an intellectual prostitute, a businessman rather than a true academic in government".

Printed in the United States
By Bookmasters